HOLLYWOOD'S ITALIANS

HOLLYWOOD'S ITALIANS

FROM PERIPHERY TO PROMINENTI

Salvatore J. LaGumina

\<teneo\> //press
AMHERST, NEW YORK

Requests for permission should be directed to
permissions@teneopress.com, or mailed to:
Teneo Press
PO Box 351
Youngstown, NY 14174

Library of Congress Control Number: 2012947633

LaGumina, Salvatore J.
Hollywood's Italians: from promenti to periphery / Salvatore J. LaGumina
p. cm.
Includes bibliographical references and index
ISBN 978-1-93484-430-4

TABLE OF CONTENTS

FOREWORD

As anyone with even a passing interest or knowledge of Italian American history can attest, one of the perennial debates in both popular culture and the academy concerns the image of Italian Americans in American society. Even with two Italian Americans sitting on the Supreme Court and their fellow Italian Americans earning their way in every field of endeavor, the stereotypes seem ineradicable: the gangster and the buffoon; the long suffering grandmother in widow's weeds and the bimbo; the Latin lover and the street thug. Hollywood has often been charged (correctly) with perpetuating these stereotypes. Salvatore LaGumina's *Hollywood's Italians* offers instead an encyclopedic compendium on the history of Italian Americans in the dream factory of Hollywood images.

Historical coincidence decreed that the mass wave of Italian immigration to the United States would occur just when motion picture industry was beginning. While some Italian immigrants may have had experience in the local theaters or traveling troupes that traced their lineage back to the Middle Ages, many Italian Americans who found their way to Hollywood had no previous acting history. That they succeeded at all is a testament to their perseverance and talent.

Although eastern European Jews may have dominated the scenes behind the camera as studio executives, no ethnic group was as prominent as the Italians in front of the camera as actors, behind the camera as directors, beside the camera as writers (or behind the set as laborers and craftsmen).

Avoiding the sometimes sterile and by now often futile debate concerning stereotypes, *Hollywood's Italians* is instead an act of loving archeology: digging in the past and assembling a colorful kaleidoscopic mosaic of tesserae. It is a pointillist portrait of a collective community. Each chapter is devoted to a theme, be it Italians who made their way to Hollywood, the transition from stage to screen, the symbiotic interaction between television and film, music on the screen, food and family, and peopled with dozens of mini-biographies that reveal often surprising bits of information. The appendix, listing all Italian American Academy Award winners and nominations, is invaluable as a historical document.

Readers will bask in the wonderful nostalgia while being simultaneously entertained and enlightened.

– Stanislao G. Pugliese
Professor of History
Queensboro Unico Distinguished Professor
of Italian and Italian American Studies
Hofstra University

HOLLYWOOD'S ITALIANS

Introduction

The creative art form of the cinema world, which embodies a matchless ability to entertain, to dramatize, and to instruct, has been part of the American experience for over a century, a time that coincided with the coming of tens of millions of newcomers representing a cross section of the diverse racial, religious, national and ethnic strains that collectively constituted those dissimilarities, distinctions and discrepancies among human beings which have enriched the American experiment. In his highly regarded book on the subject of movies, *How to Read a Film*, James Monaco identifies movies as making a critical difference in whether or not that art form mirrors or encourages trends in society. "Film has changed the way we perceive the world and therefore, to some extent, how we operate in it. ... Historians argue whether the movies simply reflected the national culture that already existed or whether they produced a fantasy of their own that eventually came to be accepted as real. In a sense the point is moot."[1] Undoubtedly, writers, directors, and producers used real-life experiences in filmmaking and therefore were not deliberately distorting, yet the very fact of amplifying certain aspects while ignoring or attenuating others could not help but shape attitudes and mores.

The invention of the motion picture machine occurred during the period historians of immigration label Mass Immigration, an era commencing roughly in the late 1880s and continuing, though interrupted by economic vicissitudes and outbreak of war, to the early 1920s. The Mass Immigration era is identified, furthermore, with large numbers of arrivals from southern, central, and eastern Europe, that is, with an influx of

Russian Jews, Greeks, Poles, Austrians, and Italians—bearers of cultures with which typical Americans had had limited contact, and consequently were very susceptible to stereotyping. To many native-born Americans or descendants from northwestern European cultures, these newcomers looked different, dressed differently, spoke differently, cooked differently, and appeared to worship differently—even in those instances where Catholic newcomers shared the same religion as substantial groups of earlier arrivals. Although the flow of immigration from Eastern Europe was quite substantial, it was Italian immigrants who came to represent the largest single cohort of new arrivals during this period as their numbers broke immigration records during the first quarter of the twentieth century. It was an influx, however, accompanied by a virulent xenophobia.[2] Though predominantly Catholic, their style of worship, customs, expressions, and outlook seemed at variance with those of fellow Catholics as, for example, the Irish.

How Hollywood treated Italians and their descendents in American society, and conversely, the extent to which they impacted American cinematic content, is the focus of this volume. The guiding principle is to demonstrate where Italian and Italian American actors, directors, producers, screenwriters, songwriters, and the like became factors in the American cinema industry and the influence of their participation. In this work, the term Italian American refers to individuals whose ancestry is wholly or partially Italian and whose names may or may not be Italian. Consequently, while many names are familiar others may be surprising if not startling and astonishing. Parenthetically, it should be added that every effort has been made to corroborate the ethnic authenticity of those included in this monograph. Eschewing an encyclopedic claim, this monograph seeks instead to shed light on the role, influence, effect, and contribution of Italian Americans in the making of films. This involves a rigorous effort to deal with Italian Americans as actors in principal and subordinate roles, as directors, producers, writers, screenwriters, composers of musical scores, and others. Accordingly, this survey provides a selective coverage of these elements of American film.

While some extant works deal with aspects of Italian American participation in the film field, the present work is unique in its distinctive coverage of selective areas that form chapters of the book: e.g., born in Italy; from stage to screen; the Italian American songbook; cuisine, comedy, character actors; and Academy Award winners. In this regard, *Hollywood's Italians* underscores the reality that Italian American interaction with filmdom goes far beyond the *Godfather* concept that is too readily accepted as summarizing Italian American contributions to the motion picture industry. Not only does their influence extend into all aspects of the field, but also, whereas they appeared on the periphery in an earlier period, in a couple of generations they have become dominant—almost indispensable—factors.

ENDNOTES

1. James Monaco, *How to Read a Film* (New York: Oxford University Press, 2000), 262.
2. For more on this topic see Salvatore J. LaGumina, *Wop!: A Documentary History of Anti-Italian Discrimination* in *the United States* (San Francisco, Straight Arrow Press, 1973). See also David J. Goldberg, chap. 7 in *Discontented America, The United States in the 1920s* (The Johns Hopkins University Press, 1999).

CHAPTER 1

BORN IN ITALY, MADE IN HOLLYWOOD

FROM VALENTINO TO VALLI

From its infancy, when it produced short films during the silent screen era, to the advent of full-length talking pictures, America's burgeoning movie industry coincided with the period of this country's greatest immigration surge, thereby assuring that the medium would be momentous for newcomers to this land of opportunity. Because Italian immigrants represented the largest cohort among all newcomers in the late-nineteenth and early-twentieth centuries they could not help but be impacted by the expanding filmmaking industry.

Shortly after he invented the phonograph, the great American inventor Thomas A. Edison filed a caveat with the Patents Office in 1888, to create a device that that would "do for the eye what the phonograph does for the ear," that is, record and reproduce objects in motion.[1] He called the apparatus a Kinetoscope, using the Greek words *kineto* meaning movement and *scopos* meaning to watch. Within a few years—in 1893—he demonstrated his first motion picture, a short scene of one of his employees pretending to sneeze. Two young, American inventors, Francis Jenkins and Thomas Armat, developed a film projector called the Vitascope that further advanced Edison's motion picture project—one that led to the first motion pictures shown to audiences in an American "movie theater," presented on April 23, 1896, in New York City.

Although United States film production would come to dwarf output in all other nations, the moviemaking industry had in fact surfaced in virtually every European country. In France, Antoine Lumière considered the potential of motion pictures when he watched a demonstration of Edison's Kinetoscope in Paris in 1892.[2] Antoine's sons Auguste and Louis Lumière patented a number of significant improvements, including the cinematographe, in 1895, that led to their development of a camera that used film perforations as a means of advancing the film through the camera and projector. That same year, they filmed the first footage ever to be recorded—takes that showed workers leaving through the front gate of the Lumière and Sons factory. There was much competition between inventors engaged in developing the motion picture machine and accordingly credit could be extended to more than one person. Thus whereas Edison's 1892 machine was limited in that a single take could be watched only by one person, adherents of French inventors cite the Lumiere product as an improvement over existing technology.

The filmmaking industry in Italy would emerge slightly later than such developments in France. Building on Edison's invention, in 1895 Italian inventor Filoteo Alberini obtained his patent for the *Kinetografo* for taking pictures, and began to charge admission to see them. Between 1903 and 1908, three movie businesses had been formed—the Roman Cines, Ambrosio of Turin and Italia Film. The businesses, which would soon be joined by other companies, produced movies for public viewing in Italy and abroad. Many of these films were historical in nature e.g., *The Capture of Rome* (1905), *Gli Ultimi Giorni di Pompei* (1908), as well as biographical accounts of the lives of Nero, Messalina, Spartacus, Julius Caesar, and others. Among the Italian actresses who became famous during this era were Lydia Borelli, Francesca Bertini, and Pina Menichelli. Apparently none of them came to make films in the United States.

While impressive, Italy's early cinematic production could not rival that of France or Germany, in part because of the lateness of its political unification, completed in 1870, but mostly because of France's dominance over Italian film production. Nevertheless, by 1910, the fledgling Italian film industry had established its own identity, with Italian movie studios employing writers, directors, and other personnel to create a thriving silent-film industry in the peninsula. Among a number of important movie epics produced in this period were *Cabiria* (1914), an extravagant historical epic that made its mark on the American film industry via its use of real locations in the Alps, thousands of extras, and a "tracking" shot with the camera placed on a dolly. It was believed that D.W. Griffith imitated some of these techniques in his movie *Intolerance* (1916).[3]

The outbreak of the First World War cut deeply into Italian movie production, initiating a reduction that persisted during the 1920s, ironically, even while Hollywood producers utilized Italy's resources for its filmmaking in movies like *Ben Hur* (1926). The Italian film industry slowly revived over the 1930s as it made its first talkie along with escapist comedies and musicals, usually depicting lives of wealth and leisure beyond the means of most Italians. The dominant political culture of fascism also insinuated itself into the movie business and manifested itself in the manufacture of diversionary lighthearted entertainment or propaganda vehicles.

The bulk of Italian immigrants to the United States, who arrived between the late 1880s and the early 1920s, possessed limited acquaintance with the movie business. Those who emigrated from major Italian cities were much more likely to have had the experience of viewing motion pictures than those who came from small, isolated villages which were not likely even to have electricity during this period—the large city of Messina, for example, did not have electricity until 1908. Thus, Italian immigrants did not enjoy the kind of prominence other immigrants experienced in the new medium, many of whom had a long-established theatrical tradition that conferred initial advantages. This was obviously true of newcomers from English-speaking countries and their issue, who accounted for large slices of the immigrant total and who entered the movie industry with English or Irish backgrounds. Indeed, some of their names would soon become the coin of the realm in the industry. Although some immigrants of non-English-speaking heritage, especially Russian Jews, would find a home and even attain dominance in the movie industry, it was not the case for Italians during the early stages. "Southern Italians did not have much success in the business of film production."[4] With the exception of Russian Jews, the new immigrant masses had little role in shaping the course of film; their cinematic representations, including plots and portrayals of characters and culture, were essentially products of Hollywood's depiction of them. "The movies and stereotypes simultaneously paraded across silver screens in small towns and big cities in America gave the nation a common fund of references and still do. ...But the signal fact of American movies has been the tenacity of Hollywood's images, genres and myths."[5] The result was that early movie renderings of the lives of Italians in Italy and Italian newcomers to these shores were cast against a stereotypical background. This was surely ironic in that, while on the one hand many cultures were deeply indebted historically to Italian culture and art in their plays and literature, yet on the other hand the embryonic movie industry largely ignored the past. A scholarly analysis of this era maintains that the racial preoccupation of early American cinema, as typified by D. W. Griffith's *The Birth of A Nation* (1916) extended to recent Italian newcomers.

> A frequently recurring measure of racial characterization was the law, with its rules and regulations defining a social contract that Italians were depicted as naturally breaking. Their allegedly "normal" relations with such criminal organizations as the Black Hand, popularized in vaudeville sketches and newspaper reports and cartoons, informed several early fictional films. ...At the same time, however, Italians were granted the possibility of redemption.[6]

The resulting ambiguity and indistinctiveness led scholar Peter Bondanella to conclude that such screen representations of Italians

> quite naturally embodied the ambivalent views of Italians that Americans of recent and much earlier vintage held of these new and colorful arrivals—they were different. …Yet, when these representations are examined carefully, they reveal a great deal of begrudging admiration, interest, and envy.[7]

Notwithstanding the fact that relatively few Italian film stars migrated to America to work in the infant moviemaking industry, the record shows that a small but appealing and committed group did make the transition, bringing with them acting experience gained in Italy. Others learned the art form here. These migrants include nineteenth-century-born male actors like Antonio Maiori, Guglielmo Ricciardi, Henry Armetta, Eduardo Cianelli, Frank Puglia, Joseph Calleia, and especially, Rudolph Valentino. A review of their careers is appropriate.

Antonio Maiori, an exceptional actor of Italian birth who was born in 1870 in Castroreale, Sicily and who studied mime and dancing in his native land, became part of a touring group that came to the United States in 1890. He soon won recognition as the most prolific producer/director in the Italian American theater and one of its leading stage performers, excelling particularly in Shakespearean roles. His depiction of Shylock from *The Merchant of Venice* prompted a critic to describe him as "the bright particular star," whose like he had not previously encountered.

> We do not recall having seen any Shylock who struck us as being quite so jovial as this one… which if it does not eclipse the recent Mansfield and Adler productions, apparently serves its purpose in giving younger Italy some sort of perspective on English drama.[8]

As impressive as his stage appearances were, Maiori's role in movies was very limited—he apparently featured in only one film of the silent screen era, *Poor Little Peppina* (1916), in which he portrayed Soldo, a Mafioso murderer and kidnapper of Lois, a young girl played by Hollywood favorite Mary Pickford, whom he spirits away to Italy. After living in Italy with Soldo and his wife, played by Concetta Arcamone, (Maiori's wife in real life) she finally escapes and he is caught. Antonio Maiori died in Brooklyn in 1938.[9]

Among the first actors transplanted from Italy to the United States was Guglielmo Ricciardi, who was born in Naples in 1879 and came to New York in 1889, where he formed the Italian Comedy-Drama Acting Company. Together with other Italian-born actors, he performed in Little Italies in various eastern cities regaling not only Italian-speaking audiences but also English-speaking viewers. Ricciardi attracted the attention of Hollywood with his work in a Luigi Pirandello play, *Come Tuo Mi Voi,* which led to a Hollywood contract to reprise his role in the film version, titled *As You Desire Me* (1932), in which he appeared together with renowned stars Greta Garbo, Melvyn Douglas and Erich von Stroheim. He also enjoyed enormous success as a character actor in the following films: *Under Two Flags* (1936), *Stars Over Broadway* (1935), *San Francisco* (1936), and *Treat 'Em Rough* (1942).

A motion-picture acting career seemed unlikely for fourteen-year-old Enrico "Henry"Armetta, born in Palermo, Sicily in 1888, who entered America in 1902 as a stowaway and who was promptly seized by authorities intent on deporting him. About to be returned to Italy, he was fortunate in that a fellow Italian came forward to sponsor him, thereby allowing him to remain in the country. He earned a living in New York City performing very menial tasks, until he became a pants presser at the New York Lambs Club, America's first professional theatrical club, which had been organized in 1874 by a group of actors and theater enthusiasts. It was a fortuitous job for one who evinced a strong interest in acting and it led to Armetta being cast in a minor role as a chorus member in a Richard Hitchcock play titled *A Yankee Consul.* The experience served to so whet his appetite for an acting career that Armetta moved to Hollywood, California in 1920 where he found work in movies as a stereotypical Italian, often playing a frenetic, excitable, and gesticulating barber, grocer, waiter, or restaurant owner. By the 1930s the hunch-shouldered, leftward tilting, mustachioed, immigrant actor with heavily-laden, Italianized, fractured English had become such a popular favorite that he was given extraneous bit roles to suit his screen persona. In the Laurel and Hardy movie *The Devil's Brother* (1933), for instance, Armetta was cast as a flustered innkeeper who worries excessively as he struggles to cope with their simplistic antics. During the 1930s he starred in a short-lived series of films about auto racing and several short story films. Sometimes playing in uncredited roles, Armetta appeared in over 152 films, including at least twenty-four films in 1934 alone; and a more substantial role in *A Bell For Adano* (1945). He also performed on stage and it was during a performance of *Opening Night,* in which he starred, that he died backstage at the relatively young age of fifty-seven—in the audience was his son John.[10]

Born in Ischia, Italy, in 1889, Eduardo Cianelli became a medical doctor like his father before him and worked briefly as a physician. However, his real passion was for grand opera and the dramatic stage. For a time, he enjoyed success in Italy as a baritone, singing in La Scala, the famed Milan Opera House, as well as opera houses throughout Europe. He immigrated to America in the early 1920s, where he appeared in Broadway musicals as well as stage dramas. He achieved acclaim reprising some of these roles in films such as *Reunion in Vienna* (1933) and *Winterset* (1936). This was the beginning of a long career in which Cianelli appeared in some 150 films, the more memorable of which were *Super Sleuth* (1937), *Gunga Din* (1939), *Bulldog Drummond's Bride* (1939), and *Foreign Correspondent* (1940). In addition, he appeared as a sinister villain in the serial *Mysterious Dr. Satan* (1940), a role that typecast him for future Hollywood productions. For example, his resemblance to racketeer Lucky Luciano led to casting Cianelli as the eloquent but deadly gangster in the aforementioned *Winterset* and a similar role in *Marked Woman* (1937). Refusing to be permanently typecast, he performed the role of a lovable, effusive, Italian speakeasy owner in *Kitty Foyle* (1940), a part for which he received an Oscar nomination. In the post–World War II era, Ciannelli returned to Italy, appearing in European films and stage productions, with occasional trips to Hollywood for movie roles. He died in Rome in 1968 and was survived by his wife and two sons.

Sicilian-born Frank Puglia (1892–1975) joined a traveling operetta company at age thirteen to begin a theatrical career, which he continued to follow upon emigration to New York, in 1907, at age fifteen. While working in a laundry, he taught himself English by reading newspapers, joined an Italian-language theater group in New York, and acted in numerous stage plays, including playing the role of Pierre Frochard in a revival of an old theatrical play, *The Two Orphans*. His performance as Frochard so impressed famed movie director D. W. Griffith that he signed him to a contract in 1921. Griffith had Puglia reprise his role for his film, retitled *Orphans of the Storm*. Interestingly, although Pierre Frochard was scripted to die at the end of the film, the preview-audience reaction to the death proved to be so negative that the final scenes were reshot, allowing Puglia to fade out. This was the beginning of an extensive Hollywood career, in which Puglia appeared in 152 films playing ethnic roles, as well as frequently being cast as a priest, a diplomat, and a musician.

While most of his screen appearances were minor they were frequently memorable, as, for example, his role as a Moroccan rug merchant who automatically marks down his prices to any friends of Rick Blaine (Humphrey Bogart) in *Casablanca* (1942). Other effectual roles in which he was cast included Joe Borelli in *Always in My Heart* (1942), Prince Cassim in *Ali Baba and the Forty Thieves* (1944), Japanese Prince Tatsugi in *Blood On The Sun* (1945), and Papa Stavros in *Girls, Girls, Girls,* (1962). Frank Puglia died in South Pasadena, California in October 1975.

Born in Italy as Rodolfo Alfonso Raffaello Piero Filiberto Guglielmi, Rudolph Valentino had a troubled childhood. His father, who had been a performer in a traveling circus before marrying and settling down, resorted to strict discipline in an effort to keep his son Rudolph in line—an effort frustrated by the boy's mother, a French woman who doted on her "beautiful baby," with the result that Rudolph became an undisciplined, pampered, bully and was expelled from many schools. He emigrated to

New York City at age eighteen in 1913—a near-record year for Italian immigration—where ill luck continued to plague him, forcing him to spend some time wandering in the streets and supporting himself with odd jobs, such as bussing tables in restaurants and gardening, before he found work as a dancer. By 1917 Valentino had become part of an operetta company which moved to California, where he began to act bit parts in silent movies, while also working as a dance teacher to wealthy women who became infatuated with him. After a couple of years playing "cabaret parasite" parts he got his big break in a 1921 movie titled *The Four Horsemen of the Apocalypse* (1921), a film that became a commercial and critical success—one of the first films to earn over a million dollars.[11]

Valentino was well on his way to becoming the epitome of the legendary, handsome, exotic, and daring Romeo, the Latin Lover who would set the standard for the mythic, amorous icon in film for years to come. Bondanella has a fascinating chapter in his study *Hollywood Italians* that discusses the power of Valentino's Latin Lover image, an image that was burnished by a series of films like *The Conquering Power* (1921), *The Sheik* (1921), *Blood and Sand* (1922), *The Eagle* (1925), and *Son of the Sheik* (1926). "He had the poise of a panther but the physique of a man who diligently worked out, often with a personal trainer, long before body building became fashionable."[12]

In Valentino, Hollywood effectively created the Latin Lover model, successfully casting him in mesmerizing performances which consciously promoted his appeal as the

> outsider, the stranger, the foil to the American movie heroes of the time...so honorable and such straight shooters that they became slightly boring. In contrast, Valentino projects an image of seductive charm, sexual prowess, and physical action—or at least a hint of it. The fact that he was not the rugged, all-American boy type who would kiss the horse rather than the girl, wore exquisite costumes beautifully, moved with the grace of a ballet dancer, but displayed a splendid physique and performed action sequences

like a trained athlete, negated the male image of the Anglo-Saxon popular at the time.[13]

Valentino's early death—he was only thirty-one when he died in 1926—assured that he would remain in the minds of moviegoers as the enduring paradigm of the Latin Lover.[14]

It might be a stretch to call Joseph Calleia—born Giuseppe Maria Spurrin-Calleja in Malta in 1897—Italian born. However, the barren but historically important island, lying in the Mediterranean Sea between Italy and Africa, which has been the crossroads of many cultures and languages, has its deepest connection with Italy. Thus, although there is an extant Maltese language, much of its literature is written in Italian. Furthermore, its location—only sixty miles from Sicily—leads to frequent interaction between Italians and inhabitants of the island and explains why Maltese islanders share so much of Italy's culture, cuisine, religion and customs as to be considered Italian in the public mind.

Educated in Maltese parochial schools (St. Julian and St. Aloysius) Joseph was inclined to the field of entertainment. He started out as a singer with a harmonic band that played first throughout Europe and then in America, where he turned to drama and appeared in many Broadway stage shows in the 1920s and 1930s. He also resorted to a variety of unusual jobs to make ends meet: washing streetcars, stoking furnaces and selling pianos to disinterested Brooklynites.[15] In 1931, Joseph went to Holly-wood, where he signed a contract to act in films, beginning with his role as a believable, menacing villain in *My Sin* (1931). It was the beginning of a remarkable career, in which appeared in fifty-seven films as a character actor, frequently playing cops or villains in gangster and western films. Over the course of a long career he played with some of Hollywood's greatest personalities, such as W.C. Fields and Mae West in *My Little Chickadee* (1940), Gary Cooper and Ingrid Bergman in *For Whom The Bells Toll* (1943), Anna Magnani and Anthony Quinn in *Wild is the Wind* (1957), and John Wayne and Richard Widmark in *The Alamo* (1960).

Calleia was a fine, multi-dimensional actor who on occasion went against his screen persona type, as illustrated by his portrayal of Buldeo, an old man who tells a tourist about the young jungle boy who was orphaned and raised by wolves in the popular film *The Jungle Book* (1942). While on the Broadway stage, his acting had caught the eye of actor/director Orson Welles who, years later, cast him as a vulnerable, understanding, policeman friend of a corrupt sheriff in his movie *A Touch of Evil* (1958), which starred Orson Welles, Charlton Heston and Janet Leigh. Calleia retired to his beloved Malta in 1963 and left an impression on people like so many character actors—his face was familiar to filmgoers who did not know his name. Asked about it, he is reputed to have replied, "Everyone recognizes my face, but no one knows my name." But astute filmmakers were well-enough aware of his exceptional talent that they sought him for their films. Francis Ford Coppola, for instance, tried, but was unable to coax Calleia out of retirement for the part of Don Corleone in his blockbuster movie, *The Godfather* (1972). The Maltese people also realized that, in Joseph Calleia, they had produced one of the finest character actors on the screen, a comprehension that prompted them to start a Joseph Calleia fan club that even continued in existence for years after his death in 1975, at age seventy-eight, and his interment in the family vault at Santa Maria Addolorata Cemetery. In 1997 the government of Malta issued a set of two stamps in his honor.

Several Italian-born actors who became exceedingly popular in Italy were accomplished athletes who projected the image of the Continental Lover that had become a veritable stereotype internationally. Rossano Brazzi, who was born in 1919 in Bologna, Italy, was a fine college athlete who participated in a variety of sports, particularly soccer and amateur boxing. The son of a shoemaker who later owned a leather factory, Rossano also became a law student, seriously studying the profession until fascists killed his parents during the Mussolini era. By the 1940s he had turned to acting, where his striking classical face as well as his ability propelled him to the heights of Italian cinema. Notwithstanding his busy acting career, he also became involved in the anti-Fascist resistance movement. He starred in dozens of movies and television shows made in various countries before his arrival in Hollywood in 1949, where he remained for years. Rossano possessed consistent and formidable acting skills, evident in his ability to so effectively transform himself into a character, rather than bend the character to himself, that one did not realize he was doing it. Accordingly, he became fairly prominent in the moviemaking capital and in international cinema, especially in the 1950s. He embodied the good-looking, middle-aged, Continental Lover type memorably as he pursued Katharine Hepburn in the elegant film *Summertime* (1955), and in the lead role in the romantic movie (with the Academy Award winning song by the same title) *Three Coins in the Fountain* (1954). Brazzi's next Holly-wood project found him launching an effort that landed him the coveted role of Emile de Becque in the big hit *South Pacific* (1958), which further cemented his image as the suave and debonair leading man. Convinced that he possessed the voice to do justice to the role's vocal dimensions by actually singing the melodies of Rodgers and Hammerstein in the movie, in the end he had to settle for the dubbing-in of the voice of the great operatic bass Giorgio Tozzi, whose glorious singing performance added to the movie's sparkle.[16] In later life, Brazzi kept busy playing character roles, mostly in European films, until the late 1980s and altogether acted in and/ or directed over 230 films, as well as maintaining a presence in Italy as an accomplished stage actor. He died in Rome in 1994.

Considered one of Italy's greatest actors and an outstanding athlete, Vittorio Gassman, born in 1922 in Genoa to a wealthy family of German origin, studied professional acting in Rome's reputable Academy of Dramatic Arts and was soon acknowledged as one of Italy's finest stage actors for his performances in Shakespearean plays—at one time in his career he started a travelling repertory company that toured Italy. In 1943 he began his filmmaking career and came to epitomize the quintessential Italian leading man: tall, dark, and handsome. He made films both in Italy and abroad, including the United States, where he parlayed his good looks, natural charisma and exceptional fluency in English into appearances in many films. Of a philosophical bent of mind, he saw the actor as a study in contradiction: "A totally healthy actor is a paradox. ...Acting is not that far from mental disease: An actor works on splitting his character into others. It is like a kind of schizophrenia." Gassman was a versatile actor whose performances ranged from classical to comedic and whose American-produced films included *The Glass Wall* (1953), *The Nude Bomb* (1980), and *Sleepers* (1996). A father of four, Gassman was married three times—one of his wives was American actress Shelly Winters—and died in Rome in the year 2000 at age seventy-seven. He was survived by his third wife, Diletta D'Andrea and his children.

Raf Vallone's mother was of an aristocratic lineage while his father was a prominent lawyer. He was born to them in 1916, in Calabria, Italy. A natural athlete who played semi-professional soccer, Raf attended the University of Turin, where he earned degrees in law and philosophy before entering his father's law firm. He then worked as a sports reporter and drama critic during World War II, while also serving with the anti-Fascist resistance movement. Vallone's Italian moviemaking career, which began in the 1940s, elevated him to the peak of popularity in the 1950s and served to introduce him to American audiences in films like *A View From The Bridge* (1952), in which he played the Italian American longshoreman Eddie Carbone, who was possessed by a desire for his niece. He had a major role in the historical epic *El Cid* (1962), and in *The Secret Invasion* (1964), *Nevada Smith* (1966), and *Godfather III* (1990). Raf was married for fifty-two years to Italian actress Elena Varzi who, along with two children, survived him upon his death in 2002.

Still another Italian actor with outstanding athletic skills was Raoul Bova, born in 1971 to Calabrian parents residing in Rome, who became a swimming champion at age sixteen. As a young man, he embarked on an acting career which saw him making television shows and movies and becoming an Italian sex symbol—a persistent Italian stereotype that he decries as not true to life and from which he is gradually moving away. A married man with three children, Bova is a relative newcomer to the American film industry whose movie American output is understandably limited—it includes key roles in *Under the Tuscan Sun* (2003), and *The Tourist* (2010), both set in Italy.

In addition to the Italian-born Hollywood male actors cited above there were also a number of Italian-born women who had distinguished Hollywood careers as actresses, including Mimi Aguglia, Argentina Brunetti, Esther Minciotti, Augusta Ciotti, Renata Vanni, Alida Valli, Anna Maria Pierangeli, Marisa Pavan, Valentina Cortese, Gina Lollobrigida, Monica Vitti, Sophia Loren, Anna Marie Alberghetti, and Isabella Rossellini.

Few have better claim to having been born to the theatrical business than Mimi Aguglia—she was literally born on the stage in Catania, Sicily, in 1884, while her pregnant mother, Giuseppina Aguglia, was playing Desdemona in William Shakespeare's *Othello*. By the time she was five, Mimi did warm up acts for her mother; by sixteen years of age she was given supporting and leading roles and went on tour in Italy, Europe, the United States, and South America. At age eighteen she married Baron Vincenzo Ferrau, a Sicilian nobleman. Upon her mother's death her father remarried a woman with whom Mini did not get along, thereby setting the stage for Mimi's momentous decision to take her younger siblings with her to the United States, where she would continue her acting career.[17]

Together with theatrical colleagues, Mimi Aguglia founded the first Sicilian Theatrical Company, which performed plays in the Sicilian dialect. She then began to use Spanish to introduce herself to a wider audience, not only in Spain, but also in Latin America, thereby establishing herself as an internationally famous actress by the time she came to this country. In the United States she performed character roles in movies including several in which she played Spanish or South American duennas and Native Americans. The legendary and eccentric industrialist and occasional producer/director Howard Hughes, citing the extraordinary impression Mimi had made on his mother, who had seen her perform in a play, personally invited her to play Jane Russell's aunt in *The Outlaw* (1943).[18] Among other well-known English film roles she played were Jean Peters' duenna in *Captain From Castile* (1947), Mario Lanza's mother in *The*

Midnight Kiss (1949), and Mama Rico in *The Brother's Rico* (1957). She also appeared in *The Man Who Cheated Himself* (1950), *Right Cross* (1950), *When in Rome* (1952), in which her daughter Argentina Brunetti was also cast, and *The Rose Tattoo* (1955).

Argentina Ferrau Brunetti, daughter of Mimi Aguglia and also a film actress, was born in Buenos Aires in 1907 and remained active until her death at age ninety-eight in 2005. She made her first stage appearance at age three and over the course of her long career played character-actress parts in over 150 films and television shows. Brunetti was hired by MGM Studios to dub the voices of such stars as Norma Shearer and Jeanette MacDonald for the Italian versions of their films. Of her movie parts, she was best known for her role as the worried Italian immigrant Mrs. Martini in the perennial favorite *It's a Wonderful Life* (1946). She also had other memorable mother roles: Ma Romano, mother of a young delinquent (John Derek) in the tense drama *Knock on Any Door* (1949), Dean Martin's mother in *The Caddy* (1953), in which he sings "That's Amore" to her, and the mother of the gangster and actor George Raft (Ray Danton) in *The George Raft Story* (1961). Brunetti was also a writer, and the cofounder of the Hollywood Foreign Press Association, in which capacity she interviewed film stars for weekly Voice of America broadcasts in Italy and Europe. She wrote a weekly column for Italian-language journals in the United States, Canada, and Italy. Argentina died at age ninety-eight in 2005, just after she completed her autobiographical novel of the family's show-business history.

Another female movie actress of Italian birth was Esther Minciotti, who was born in Italy in 1883 and died in Jackson Heights, Queens in 1962. She usually played the mother role as, for example, Theresa Monetti in *House of Strangers* (1949), who was compelled to contend with her difficult husband Gino (Edward G. Robinson) whose illegal activities alienated two of his three sons. She likewise played the role of Mme. Maria Caraffa in *Strictly Dishonorable* (1951), Mama Pauletta Rocco in *Full of Life* (1956), and Mama Balestrero in *The Wrong Man* (1956). Her most distinguished mother role was in the Academy Award–winning movie *Marty* (1955), in which she played a mother who constantly nags her son Marty Piletti (Ernest Borgnine), the unpretentious, lonely butcher in his late thirties whose bachelorhood is beginning to weigh heavily on the family. In playing the role of Marty's mother Esther Minciotti embodies the stereotypical Italian mother figure. "The old-woman-as-mamma is always dressed in black because she is always widowed and is circum-scribed within an obsessive concern for her son."[19] She is worried he will never marry and is torn between encouraging him to go on dates and giving in to her doubts that that outcome would be the best thing for her. Her performance won the praise of *New York Times* critic Bosley Crowther "As the disquieted mother of the hero, Esther Minciotti is superb, and Augusta Ciolli is devastating as a grimly dependent aunt."[20]

Playing the role of Aunt Catherine in *Marty*, Augusta Ciolli, who was born in 1901 and died in New York in 1967, goes directly and devastat-ingly to the point as a grimly reliant aunt when she equates her status of an aging aunt to excess household baggage:

> So I'm an old garbage bag put in the street, huh?… These are the worst years, I tell you. It's going to happen to you. I'm afraid to look in a mirror… I'm afraid I'm gonna see an old lady with white hair, just like the old ladies in the park with little bundles and black shawls waiting for the coffin. I'm fifty-six years old. And what am I gonna do with myself? I've got strength in my hands. I want to clean. I want to cook. I want to make dinner for my children. Am I an old dog to lay near the fire till my eyes close? These are terrible years, Theresa, terrible years… It's gonna happen to you. It's gonna happen to you!

Interestingly, Augusta Ciolli was only fifty-four years of age when *Marty* was filmed. In *Love With The Proper Stranger* (1963) Ciolli played the role Mrs. Papasano, mother of Rocky Papasano (Steve McQueen).

Renata Vanni, born in Naples, Italy, in 1909, started her career in Italian theater and then moved to Italian-language radio in New York. She signed a contract with Warner Brothers in the late 1940s, and was given supporting roles in dozens of movies, including *A Patch of Blue* (1965), *Pay or Die* (1960), and *Wait Until Spring Bandini* (1989). One of the most interesting pictures in which she was cast in a strong supporting role was *Westward the Women* (1951) in which she played Signora Moroni, an Italian widow. In this unusual film, written by Frank Capra and directed by William Wellman, 140 women pioneers travel from Chicago to California in 1851 as mail-order brides for workers on a California farm where there is a severe shortage of women. An atypical western, it revolves around a tale that celebrates the courage and the trials experienced by those early pioneer women without whom the West could not have advanced. Renata plays a northern-Italian immigrant who, along with other women, endures danger, pain and grueling hardship before reaching their destination. There, fortuitously, she meets an Italian immigrant man from the same region, who shares a similar heritage and with whom she can converse in the familiar Old World tongue.[21] Renata appeared in several live television shows and soon became a familiar face in episodic television shows such shows as *Gunsmoke*, *The Love Boat* and *The Mod Squad*, as well as playing a recurring role as Marlo Thomas' landlady on *That Girl*. Renata Vanni died in 2004 in California and was survived by her daughter, actress Delia Salvi, who is also a professor at UCLA's Film and Television Department.

Alida Valli (sometimes credited simply as Valli) was born in Pola, Italy (today part of Croatia) in 1921, to parents of mixed Austrian-Italian ancestry. She was the bearer of an aristocratic legacy and a title conferred upon her at her christening: Baroness von Marckenstein und Frauenberg. By the 1940s, the dark-haired beauty with an aristocratic face had become one of Italy's favorite female movie stars whose blue eyes, chestnut hair and refined features were acknowledged internationally. A former theater student at Rome's Film School, she was highly regarded as an actress in Europe, where she was compared to the likes of Marlene Dietrich and Greta Garbo, and was on the verge of signing a Hollywood contract when World War II intervened. In 1947 she was signed to a contract by David

Selznick, who saw her as a successor to Ingrid Bergman.[22] Even as she began to learn the language, she began making English-language movies, the most notable of which was the courtroom drama, *The Parradine Case* (1947), in which she played Maddalena Paradine, an enigmatic, young, foreign woman living in London, who is suspected of murdering her blind husband. She was also cast as a mysterious Czech refugee in the visually stylish film-noir thriller *The Third Man* (1949) set in decadent and rotting Vienna at the conclusion of World War II. She also appeared in *The Miracle of the Bells* (1948), and *Walk Softly, Stranger* (1950). She spent most of her moviemaking career in Europe where, as one of the most enduring actresses, she appeared in over one hundred films. She was married to composer Oscar De Mejo with whom she had two sons before her divorce, and she died in 2006 at age eighty-four.

Born in Calgari, Sardinia in 1932, twin sisters Anna Maria Pierangeli and Marisa Pavan began their careers acting in Italian motion pictures, including one with Vittorio De Sica. Pier Angeli, as she was more commonly known, came to the United States when she was eighteen to make her American movie debut in *Teresa* (1951), a psychological melodrama of a young, vacillating, American soldier who marries Teresa Russo (Pier Angeli) and brings her to the United States to live with him and his parents, whereupon the marriage begins to crumble. Pier Angeli elicited rave reviews for her poignant, sensitive and sincere performance, for which she won a Golden Globe Award, and which led one critic to compare her to legendary actress Greta Garbo. *Somebody Upstairs Likes Me* (1956) and *Code Name Red Roses* (1969), were among the other Hollywood films in which she starred.

The petite and lovely doe-eyed actress with a beautiful smile was said to have been in love with James Dean and Kirk Douglas but she married popular singer Vic Damone and had a son named Perry with him. However, the marriage was short-lived. The failure of a second marriage and the emotional strain from depression took its toll—in 1971, thirty-nine-year-old Pier was found dead of a barbiturate overdose in her Beverly

Hills home. In the last year of her life she had returned to the faith of her youth and her grieving family and many Hollywood personalities were at her funeral Mass at the Roman Catholic Church of the Good Shepard.[23]

Born Marisa Pierangeli in Cagliari, Sardinia, Italy, Marisa, the twin sister of Pier Angeli, came to America in 1952 and became a Hollywood actress in the 1950s, appearing in supporting roles in several films, including *What Price Glory?* (1952), *The Man in the Gray Flannel Suit* (1955), and *Diane* (1956). Her most notable role was as the hot-blooded, virginal daughter Rosa Delle Rose in *The Rose Tattoo* (1955), for which she received the Best Supporting Actress nomination. Marisa also worked as an actress in television dramas. She was twice married to French actor Jean-Pierre Aumont until his death in 2001, and she had two children with him.[24]

Born in Milan, Italy in 1925, Valentina Cortese became a well known, very competent, actress whose beauty and gentle and sweet persona led to her making movies as a teenager in her home country, often in ingénue parts. Valentina then made movies in England, including *The House on Telegraph Hill* (1951), a gripping suspense thriller set amidst the shambles of wartorn Europe, in which she displays winning appeal as a death camp survivor and displaced person. One of the fascinating aspects of this role was that she played with Richard Basehart, whom she married and with whom she had a son before divorcing. Over the course of her long career, Cortese appeared in many films made in Europe and in Hollywood, such as *Black Magic* (1949 and *The Barefoot Contessa* (1954). She also worked extensively in television. Movie critic Vincent Canby considered Valentina's role as an aging film star in *Day for Night* (1973) her screen performance highlight. "The performances are superb. Miss Cortese and Miss Bisset are not only both hugely funny but also hugely affecting, in moments that creep up on you without warning."[25] Her role in the film won her an Oscar nomination for Best Supporting Actress.

During the immediate post–World War II period a bevy of Italian-born actresses became part of the American cinema scene for at least part of their careers. La Lollo, as the Italians called Gina Lollobrigida, was the first postwar Italian actress to achieve stardom.[26] Born into a poor working-class family in 1927 as Luigina Lollobrigida, in Subiaco, Italy, Gina's career went off like a rocket after participating in an Italian beauty contest—her beguiling, sultry looks and curvaceous figure, even her capriciousness, attracted not only public attention but also film producers. Endowed with beautiful breasts, some called her the World's Most Beautiful Woman and also dubbed her a Sex Goddess. She had come to the attention of American screen fans by the 1950s. Gina's first American movie was *Beat the Devil* (1953), a story about raffish misfits en route to British East Africa in a little Italian seaport which, even though poorly received originally, has developed an increased following since then. Among other movies she made was *Trapeze* (1956), where she plays the love interest, a melodrama which received mixed reviews but which did well at the box office, and in the well-received *Buena Sera, Mrs. Campbell* (1968), in which Gina showed her ability to play comedy. In her post-movie career Gina Lollobrigida has established herself as an artist working as a sculptor as well as a skilled photographer, whose works have been seen in many exhibitions. Although romantically linked to a number of celebrities, she was married only once, to Drago Milko Skofic, whom she divorced and with whom she had a son.[27]

Monica Vitti, who was born Maria Luisa Ceciarelli in 1931 in Rome, and who was attracted to acting while performing in amateur productions as a teenager, began to train seriously at Rome's National Academy of Dramatic Arts. She appeared in many Italian films directed by Michelangelo Antonioni, usually as an icy, remote, uninvolved woman. Monica's American film work was limited, essentially only *Modesty Blaise* (1966), in which she gained recognition for going against sexual and neurotic preoccupation to become a more than active and competent intelligence operative in spiked heels—a female version of James Bond. In her later career, she worked in Italy as an actress and teacher as well as acting and directing on television. In 2000 Vitti married Roberto Russo.

Regarded as one of the twenty-five greatest American female screen legends of all time, Sophia Loren was born Sofia Villani Scicolone in Rome in 1934. She entered, and was selected as a finalist in, a beauty contest held in Naples when she was fourteen years old, soon enrolled in acting classes that led to several screen roles playing extras, and quickly abandoned her original name in favor of Loren.[28] As her star rose she began to appear in a number of films teamed with Marcello Mastroianni that gained popularity in Italy and also attracted attention in Hollywood, resulting in a contract with Paramount Pictures and in the making of a number of films with some of Hollywood's leading men, such as Gregory Peck, Paul Newman, Frank Sinatra, and Cary Grant. She also continued to make films in Italy, including Two Women (1961), a Vittorio De Sica production in which she played a mother who is raped as she tries to protect her daughter amidst the chaos of wartorn Italy. Loren's stunning, realistic performance earned the plaudits of the public and movie critics alike, who rewarded her with twenty-two acting awards, including the Academy Award for Best Actress, marking the first time *the award was proffered for* a non-English-speaking role. She also received international awards for her role in Marriage Italian Style (1964), another Italian-made movie.[29]

Among the many Hollywood films made by Sophia Loren are: *Boy on a Dolphin*, 1957), *The Pride and the Passion*, (1957), *Desire Under the Elms* (1958), *Houseboat*, 1958, and *Arabesque* (1966). In the 1960s and 1970s Loren had reached international stardom and the pinnacle of her profession by winning a second Oscar nomination and numerous other awards. In 1991 she received an Honorary Academy Award for her body of work, and was named "one of the genuine treasures of the world cinema."[30] In 1966 Sophia Loren married Italian film producer Carlo Ponti, with whom she had two sons, Carlo Jr. and Eduoardo, and lived with him in France until he died in 2007. She also started a fragrance and cosmetic eyewear business.

The child prodigy of two musicians—her father a concertmaster and opera singer, her mother a pianist—Anna Maria Alberghetti, born in Pesaro, Italy in 1936, took to music naturally and impressed European audiences with her fine soprano singing as a child. After the Alberghettis left Italy for America in the wake of the Second World War, twelve-year-old Anna made her debut in New York's prestigious Carnegie Hall, a successful start that opened doors to other distinguished orchestras, such as the New York Philharmonic, where she performed as featured soloist. She would soon be seen on television shows, especially *The Ed Sullivan Show*, which introduced Anna Maria to vast audiences, including director Frank Capra, who was so taken by her that he insisted on casting her in her first Hollywood movie: *Here Comes The Groom* (1951):

> Then there was the fourteen-year-old Italian singer. I first heard her bell-like coloratura tones bring an audience to its feet in Ed Sullivan's Sunday night TV show. I had to have her—as a singer to my soft orphanage opening, and as another 'kitchen stove' to throw into my last Paramount film.[31]

Making records and performing in stage musicals such as *West Side Story*, *The Sound of Music* and, most notably, *Carnival,* for which she won a Tony Award as the Best Actress in a Musical and which added to her popularity and led to a movie contract.[32]

Among the movies in which Anna Maria appeared are: *The Medium* (1951), *10,000 Bedrooms* (1957), *Cinderfella* (1960), and *The Whole Shebang* (2001). To some, these films, while entertaining, did not make the best use of her talents. However, her popularity was such that her picture was on the cover of *Life* magazine on May 5, 1961. Although Alberghetti's marriage in 1964 to director/producer Claudio Guzman did not last, it produced two daughters who have since embarked on their own careers, thereby allowing Anna Maria to resume her career. Utilizing the gifts with which she was endowed, her training and the profession-alism born of an experience that approaches seven decades in extent, she continues to perform in theatrical productions, concerts, and lectures in a variety of venues, from town halls and colleges to Italian festivals.

The bearer of a legendary cinema name, Isabella Fiorella Elettra Giovanna Rossellini, born in Rome, Italy, in 1952, was the daughter of Italian film director Roberto Rossellini and Ingrid Bergman, the celebrated Swedish-born actress. Isabella has had a varied career, working as a translator, model, philanthropist, entrepreneur, and filmmaker in addition to working as an actress on television and in movies. Her first film appearance was in a minor role in *A Matter of Time* (1976), a film that was not regarded as a memorable production, notwithstanding the fact that her mother, Ingrid Bergman, also appeared in it. Isabella appeared in a number of other films, one of which, *Blue Velvet* (1986), is a sensual mystery that offered Isabella an opportunity to play a more dramatic part as the beautiful and mysterious nightclub singer Dorothy Vallens, caught up in a world of psycho-sexual brutality within the confines of a small town setting that reeks with morbid personalities. Although originally not highly acclaimed, the film did receive a number of awards, including one for her as the Best Female Lead and has since become a film-noir fixture. Isabella also starred in *White Nights* (1985), *Cousins* (1989), and *Death Becomes Her* (1992). She has also had roles in television shows, has done screenwriting and is committed to promoting conservation efforts. Isabella Rossellini, a citizen of both the United States and Italy, has been married and divorced twice, first with director Martin Scorsese and second with Jon Wiedemann, and has two children.[33]

The profiles of those performers treated above represent a sampling of many who have interacted with the Hollywood cinema world. The reality is that, although they are not treated in detail here, there have been, and there continue to be, dozens of Italian-born film actors and actresses who have spent parts of their careers making Hollywood movies. Among other names that can be mentioned are Milly Vitale, Fabio Lanzoni, Anna Maria Sandri, Franco Nero, Claudia Cardinale, Elissa Landi, Cesare Danova,

Virna Lisi, Isa Miranda, Luciana Paluzzi, Elsa Martinelli, Giovanna Ralli, Rosanna Schiaffino, Monica Belluci, and Daniela Bianchi.

Endnotes

1. Monaco, *How to Read a Film*, 83–88, 256–258.
2. Randall E. Stross, *The Wizard of Menlo Park: Thomas Alva Edison* (New York: Broadway, 2008) 197, 207.
3. Stross, *The Wizard of Menlo Park*, 197, 207.
4. Giorgio Bertellini, *Italy in Early American Cinema: Race, Landscape and the Picturesque* (Bloomington: Indiana University Press, 2010), 264.
5. Randall M. Miller, ed., *The Kaleidoscope Lens, How Hollywood Views Ethnic Groups* (New York: Jerome S. Ozer, 1980), 1.
6. Bertellini, Italy in Early American Cinema, 10.
7. Peter Bondanella, *Hollywood Italians* (New York: Continuum, 2004), 14.
8. *New York Times*, May 30, 1905
9. Emelise Aleandri, The Italian–American Immigrant Theater of New York City (Charleston, S.C, 1999), 36.
10. *York Times*, October 23, 1945.
11. Emily Lieder, Dark Lover, *The Life and Death of Rudolph Valentino* (New York, Faber and Faber, 2004), 4. This work empahasizes that his dark pigmentation relegated Valentino to villian roles at a time when movie heroes proferred a more All American tall-in-the-saddle look.
12. Bondanella, *Hollywood Italians*, 155. See also Bertellini, *Italy in Early American Cinema*, 206.
13. Bondanella, *Hollywood Italians*, 144.
14. Further analyses regarding the Latin "lover" image can be found in Jacqueline Reich, *Beyond The Latin Lover: Marcello Mastroianni Masculinity, and Italian Cinema* (Bloomington, Indiana University Press, 2004), xii.
15. *New York Times*, November 21, 1943.
16. Carla Celli and Marga Cottino–Jones, *A New Guide to Italian Cinema* (New York, Palgrave Macmillan, 2007), 86.
17. Aleandri, The Italian American Immigrant Theater, 59–63.
18. Argentina Brunetti, *In Sicilian Company* (Albany, Georgia, BearManor Media, 2005), 170–172.
19. Dawn Esposito, "Italian American Women in the Cinema," in *Italian American, A Retrospective on The Twentieth Century*, eds. Paola Sensi-Isolani and Anthony Julian Tamburri, (New York:American Italian Historical Association, 2001), 203–224.

20. Bosley Crowther, "Marty 1955," *New York Times*, April 12, 1955.

21. Laura E. Ruberto, "Westward the Women, " *Raccogli e passa (blog)*, July 8, 2008, http://www.i-italy.org/bloggers/3319/westward-women.

22. For an account of how Hollywood courted Valli see, Howard Taubman, "Fact Versus Fiction in the Discovery of a Star," *New York Times*, January 11, 1948.

23. Jane Allen, *Pier Angeli, A Fragile Life* (Jefferson, North Carolina: MacFarland, 2002), 2, 10.

24. Vic Damone and David Chanof, *Singing Was The Easy Part* (New York: St. Martin's Press, 2009), 138–149.

25. Vincent Canby, "*Day for Night*: Truffaut's Own World Viewed From Inside The Cast," *New York Times*, September 29, 1973.

26. Réka C. V. Buckley, "National Body: Gina Lollobrigida and the cult of the star in the 1950s." in *Historical Journal of Film, Radio &* Television, October 2000, Vol. 20, Issue 4. 527–547.

27. Robert Johnson, " Saga of a Siren, *Saturday Evening Post*, August 13, 1960, Vol. 233, Issue 7, 18–76; Luis A. Canales, *Imperial Gin: The Very Unauthorized Biography of Gina Lollobrigida* (Braden Books, 1992).

28. John Cheever, "Sophia, Sophia, Sophia," Saturday Evening Post, October 21, 1967.

29. Warren G. Harris, *Sophia Loren: A Biography* (New York: Simon & Schuster, 1998) check it out.

30. GregoryPeck, 1991 Academy Awards Presentations, March 25, 1991.

31. Frank Capra, *The Name Above the Title, An Autobiography* (New York: Macmillan and Co., 1971), 421.

32. Pete Martin, "Backstage With Anna Maria Alberghetti," *Saturday Evening Post*, Vol. 234, 96-99.

33. Isabella Rossellini, *In The Name of the Father, the Daughters and the Holy Spirits* (London: Haus Publishing, 2006). This work provides interesting information on her famous parents, their scanal and her father's dislike of Hollywood. See also *New York Times*, May 8, 2006.

CHAPTER 2

FROM STAGE TO SCREEN

Acting has been defined as a meritocratic activity, that is, a system wherein ability is the measure of quality rather than fanciful or supposed talent. Basically the former is genuine while the latter may be far-fetched or clever. Successful acting requires the participant to pretend he or she is someone else; it also requires extensive preparation within a short period of time while still having the energy to live one's own life. It is a profession that is not just about good looks but also about how one performs, how the actor exists on the stage or the film set. For professional actors, the allure of the stage is a constant, invariable magnet, one that tempts them to confront the test of performing before live audiences, an experience which presents performance challenges that are quite different from those offered by the motion picture industry. On stage it is the performance that counts, it is the setting where actors can test their skills at executing roles, the venue where they can impress and leave the audience member with the same feeling as that of a visitor to a world-renowned museum viewing a glorious and masterful portrait that exudes perfection in proportion and grace. Stage acting provides the setting where portrayals are so exquisitely burnished that audiences forget they are viewing an artificial spectacle; the site where actors must perform sharp changes of mood from abrupt expressions of anger to a more silent, reflective spirit. For those actors and actresses determined to convey plots via the story-telling medium or who seek to depict a character by speaking or singing a written text in a play—in a word, those for whom acting is in their blood —the live audience is what distinguishes theater acting from all other performances. Stage portrayals allow actors to hone a wide range of skills, including voice projection, enunciation and clarity of speech; physical expressivity; the expression of emotions; and the use of imagination, inter-pretive improvisation, and body language. While some have entered the acting profession with little or no upbringing or training in the field, it is not uncommon for aspiring actors to have some background in high school or college plays, community theater, traveling groups, and the like. The stage affords actors the opportunity to be creative and to display their talents as they compete with other actors for the limited available posi-tions. In this respect, the attraction of performing on the stage definitely applies to actors of Italian descent whether the reference is to those born in Italy who gained their initial acting experience on Italian stages, those who came with limited acting experience, or those born in this country. Even though many achieved film success, they often sought to balance it with work in live theater. While not attempting to be exhaustive, it would be useful to offer several examples.

Rafaela Ottiano, born in Venice, Italy in 1888, established herself on the Italian stage before coming to America in 1910. Eschewing the suburban lifestyle near Boston chosen by her parents and determined to become an actress, she went to New York City, where she lived in a rooming house peopled with aspiring actresses and artists who competed for scarce acting roles in theater. Although the five foot five brunette began to gain notice for her performances in numerous, small, New York theatrical productions, the efforts yielded such an inadequate income that she was compelled to augment it by working as a department store saleslady. She gained even more attention in 1924 for her role in orchestrating murder and cannibalism in *Sweeney Todd: The Demon Barber of Fleet Street*. Reprising the personification-of-evil role sixty-seven times led to her typecasting as an actress who specialized in sinister, spiteful characterizations on the stage. Thus, she played a villain in *Diamond Lil,* starring Mae West, in 1928 and reenacted the same role in the movie version, *She Done Him Wrong* (1933). She likewise played variations of loathsome and obnoxious characters in films like *The Devil Doll* (1935), and *Riffraff* (1936), as well as a more benign role in *Curly Top* (1935), and a character named Rafaela Ottiano, (actually named in her honor), in *Grand Hotel* (1932).[1]

Throughout the course of her career Rafaela worked with some of Hollywood's most famous actors, including Barbara Stanwyck, Conrad Nagel, Peter Lorre, and Shirley Temple. She never married and had no children. Treated for intestinal cancer, she died at age fifty-four in 1942 at the East Boston home of her late parents.

Anna Maria Louisa Italiano (Anne Bancroft), born in 1931 in the Bronx, New York, to Italian immigrant parents—her father was a patternmaker, and her mother a telephone operator—is another case of a film star with a stage-acting background. The Parkchester, Bronx neighborhood of Anne's birth reeked of an *italianita* in the streets, in the homes and in church picnics. As a biographer put it: "Anne grew up *una buona ragazza di famiglia,* a good girl from a good family."[2] For the Italianos it meant an extended family, numbering close to eighty, that could best be accommodated in picnic settings where four-year-old Anne would entertain an appreciative family audience by singing as her uncle played guitar. Her acting interest manifested itself in Christopher Columbus High School, where Anne became a member of the Drama Club and performed in school plays. Sensing that her daughter possessed innate acting talent, Anne's mother insisted that she attend the New York Academy of Dramatic Arts, where she learned acting techniques. In the course of time, Anne found acting work on television, briefly under the name of Ann Marno, and also, in the 1950s, in films. She later won an Academy Award for Best Actress for her work in the film version of *The Miracle Worker* (1962) and received subsequent nominations for her roles in other movies. Interrupting her movie career for Broadway theater proved hugely successful for her, as she won the prestigious Tony Award for the Best Performance by a Featured Actress in a Play in *Two for the Seesaw* (1958), her Broadway debut, in which she was paired with the prominent star Henry Fonda, and in which she played a struggling New York dancer who falls in love with Fonda, then in the process of divorcing his wife. The relationship, however, is hampered by differences in background and temperament. "Anne Bancroft walked on stage a nobody and floated off a star," was how a critic described her winning performance.[3] Her other Tony Award was for *The Miracle Worker* (1959), wherein she played Anne Sullivan, governess and teacher to the blind, deaf, mute, and wild Helen Keller. She was also nominated for a similar Tony Award for her work in the title role in *Golda* (1977), and even made the cover of the national magazine *Time*.[4]

The aforementioned Henry Fonda (1905–1982), whose Italian ancestry can be traced to northern Italy, which the Fonda family left during a time of religious upheaval in the sixteenth century, is another exceptional example of preference for the stage.[5] One of Hollywood's most acclaimed, enduring and respected actors and the recipient of numerous movie awards, he began his stage career in the late 1920s, not as an actor but as a shy young man fascinated with the backstage aspects of theater. Thus he learned everything from set construction to stage production, in which he was employed for years on theater stages in and around New York. He was attracted to acting after realizing that, his shyness notwithstanding, he could be comfortable hiding behind a writer's scripted words and playing a part other than himself—such was his unlikely preparation for Hollywood. Fonda continued his association with the stage for virtually the rest of his life, including his last two Broadway stage appearances: *Clarence Darrow* (1975), a demanding role for which he received a Tony nomination, and *First Monday* (1978).

One of Broadway's busiest and most versatile actors, Philip M. Bosco only became a widely recognized stage star in his later years. However, for decades he gave superlative performances in classic and contemporary comedies and dramas. He was born in Jersey City, New Jersey, in 1930, the son of a father who was carnival operator and a mother who was a policewoman. He went to Saint Peter's Prep School in Jersey City and was also educated in the Speech and Drama Department of Catholic University of America. His ties to New Jersey have continued as he, his wife, and their seven children remain residents of the state. At six foot one, he had the physical size and the heft to work as a truck driver before entering the world of acting.[6] Upon graduating Catholic University he was offered a seven-year film contract but refused it because he did not want to live in Hollywood, and because he preferred theater acting. Trained as a resident actor at Washington's Arena Stage, he made his Broadway debut as a kind of modern-thinking Heracles in *The Rape of the Belt* (1960), a performance that won him a nomination for a Tony Award. Philip also subsequently received Best-Actor Tony Award nominations for *Heartbreak House* (1984), *You Can Never Tell* (1987), *Moon Over Buffalo* (1996), and *Twelve Angry Men* (2005). He performed on the stage for decades in plays for Manhattan theater companies such as the New York Shakespeare Festival, the Roundabout, the Circle in the Square, and Lincoln Center. In addition, he also appeared in films, including *Requiem for a Heavyweight* (1962), *Children of a Lesser God* (1986), *Working Girl* (1988), *Kate & Leopold* (2001), *Hitch* 2005), and *The Savages* (2007).

Clearly, the stage is Bosco's first love. His Tony-winning performance in the farce *Lend Me a Tenor* (1990) was only one of many accolades he received. In 2007 one reviewer was prompted to comment; "For over forty years, Philip Bosco has been one of the crown acting jewels of Broadway Theater."[7] In addition to *Lend Me a Tenor*, his flawless talents have graced such Great White Way productions as *An Inspector Calls*, *Heartbreak*, *The Heiress*, *Twelfth Night*, and *Copenhagen*. The professionalism and variety of his performances have elicited admiration from the keenest of critics. Mel Gussow, for example, has described him "as a kind of one-man repertory company, [who] has proven that an actor can have a full, gratifying career on the New York stage."[8] Considered one of the most distinguished stage actors of his time, Bosco has received the New York Critics Circle Award and an Obie Award for Lifetime Achievement in the Theatre. In 1998, he was inducted into the Theater Hall of Fame and was the recipient of two honorary doctorates. He and his wife Nancy have seven children and fifteen grandchildren.

Tony LoBianco, born the son of a taxi driver in Brooklyn, New York in 1936, is a Golden Glove boxer who has made his mark both as a character actor and in occasional lead roles in many films, the most important of which was the Academy Award winner *The French Connection* (1971), in which he plays the role of Salvatore "Sal" Boca, a small time hood with connections to French drug dealers. Other films in which he has appeared include *The Seven Ups* (1973), *Bloodbrothers* (1978), *City Heat* (1984), and *Kill The Irishman* (2011). He has also performed on the stage making his Broadway debut in 1966 in *The Office*, and has continued to sharpen his blue collar image into that of a credible theater performer, one who has been honored by his peers by winning the OBIE Award as fading baseball star Duke Bronkowsky in the *Yanks 3 Detroit 0 Top of the Seventh* (1975–76). He has also received an Outer Critics Circle Award and a Tony nomination for his role in Arthur Miller's *A View from the Bridge* (1983). *Hizzoner,* his one-man show about the career of Fiorello H. LaGuardia, New York City's most colorful mayor, has been both criticized and applauded. While more than a few theater critics were negatively impressed with Lobianco's portrayal of LaGuardia in the stage play, he also won an Emmy Award for his role in the Public Broadcasting System's adaptation for the screen.[9] The critics who disapproved of his performance in *Hizzoner* nevertheless praised LoBianco for his acting in naturalist roles, like his performance in *A View From The Bridge*.

LoBianco has lent his stature to Italian American activities, including a stint as the national spokesman for the Order Sons of Italy in America. He also has great admiration for injured servicemen and servicewomen, whom he visits frequently in hospitals. He is married to Elizabeth LoBianco, has three daughters and lives in New York.

Al Pacino is an excellent example of someone who is a current major Hollywood actor—he has starred in Academy Award–winning films, won a Best Actor Oscar and was nominated five times for Oscars—yet has consistently succumbed to the clarion call of the stage. "Pacino feels his roots are in the theater, and he returns whenever the pressure of being a movie 'star' becomes too great," explains his biographer. [10] When asked whether or not he has more interest in plays than movies, Al's response undoubtedly reflects the sentiments of many actors whose preference for performing is the stage.

> Yes, I would say I am more concerned with the plays I am going to do than the movies. I'm more comfortable in a play. In a film there's always a certain sense of control, of holding back. The stage is different; there is more to act. There are more demands put on you, more experiences to go through. It is a different craft when it's on the stage. The play is the source. It's orchestrated with words. In a movie you are not dealing as much in that. There are machines and wires. When you're acting for a camera, it keeps taking and never giving back. When you perform with a live audience, the audience comes back to you so that you and the audience are giving to each other, in a sense. [11]

The inauspicious upbringing of the New York City–born (in 1940) future star Alfred James Pacino was compounded by the divorce of his parents and his antipathy to formal schooling. He is said to have been a troublemaker—he flunked nearly all of his classes except English and was a dropout at age seventeen. However, while in junior high school, he was voted most likely to succeed, primarily because of his acting ability. During his teenage years he had a succession of menial jobs, ranging from shining shoes to polishing fresh fruit, while he acted in off-Broadway plays, gradually insinuating himself into New York's theatrical scene while he continued to study the craft at The Actors Studio. Before he made it big in Hollywood films he worked as a stage actor throughout the 1960s in plays such as *Awake and Sing*, *America*, *Hurrah*, and *The Indian Wants the Bronx*, winning an Obie Award as Best Actor for the latter. He won Tony Awards in 1969 in his Broadway debut, *Does a Tiger Wear a Necktie?* and in 1971 for his part in *The Basic Training of Pavlo Hummel*. In 1983 he received rich compliments for his role in *American Buffalo,* a play about three lowlifes on the lowest rungs of the social ladder which reminds people that life's ambiguities can corrupt good intentions. Pacino, moreover, remains active in the theater field, teaching an acting class while continuing his live theater performances. The stage debut of his interpretation of Shylock in *The Merchant of Venice,* in 2010 at Central Park, for instance, received high praise from the critics. To many a professional actor, Pacino's theatrical talent and his relentless pursuit to portray a stage character surpass his screen performances. As the actor Ed Harris, who worked with him, put it, "Al is such a huge film star now, we tend to forget and overlook the fact that he is first and foremost a stage actor."[12]

Bernadette Peters has made some thirty-two movies and television films, among which was *Silent Movie* (1976, for which she was nominated for a Golden Globe Award), *Annie* (1982), *Pink Cadillac* (1989) and *Alice* (1990). She was cast in a role written by Steve Martin expressly for her in *The Jerk* (1979) which also garnered her a Golden Globe Award. In the recent film *Come le formiche* (2006, released in the United States as *Wine and Kisses*), which was filmed in Italy, she acts the part of a rich American who becomes involved with an Italian family that owns a vineyard.

Her film success notwithstanding, Bernadette is perhaps better known for her performances on stage, especially in musicals, for which she has received nominations for the Tony Award seven times, winning twice, and earned other prestigious wards. She was born Bernadette Lazzara in Ozone Park, Queens, New York, to an Italian American family. Her father drove a bread delivery truck while her mother Marguerite, whose unrequited acting aspirations were quashed by her own, Sicilian, mother, concentrated on Bernadette's acting talents, natural gifts which were manifested in a television show when she was three years old. She attended P.S. 58, a local elementary school. However, by nine years of age and unbeknownst to her classmates, the multitalented actress had obtained an Actors Equity Card and begun acting professionally on stage, where she went on to build up a tidy repertoire by the time she became a teenager.[13] She attended Quintano's School for Young Professionals in Manhattan—a location closer to Broadway theaters. It was at about this point in her career that her mother decided she should change her ethnic-sounding name of Lazzara to a neutral one. Critics were so pleased with her voice that they recommended her to recording companies, which steered her to the production of a number of recordings and elevated her to popular singer status before she even graduated from high school. Not surprisingly, this early vocal success presaged regular performances in off-Broadway musicals, like *Dames at Sea,* for which she won the Drama Desk Award. Her appearances on the Broadway stage brought Peters more awards: a Theater World Award for her work in *George M!* (1968) and Tony nominations for her roles in *On The Town* (1971), *Sunday in the Park with George* (1984), and *Gypsy* (2003). She earned Tony Awards for *Song and Dance* (1985), a role that led New York Times critic Frank Rich to remark that she "has no peer in the musical theater right now," and *Annie Get Your Gun* (1999). In 2010, she once again acted on the Broadway stage when she replaced Catherine Zeta-Jones in Stephen Sondheim's *A Little Night Music.* Peters is known for her charitable work on behalf of animal adoptions and has also begun to write children's books. In 2004 New York Women in Communications honored her with a Matrix Award in the Arts & Entertainment category in ceremony at the Waldorf Astoria Hotel. She married Michael Wittenberg in 1996 but lost him in helicopter accident in 2005.

Few actresses can claim a theatrical lineage that can match that of Patti Lupone, whose great-grandaunt was Adelina Patti, one of nineteenth-century Italy's most celebrated opera singers. Born in Northport, Long Island, Patti's mother was of Abruzzese heritage while her father's background was Sicilian. Because of close family ties as a youngster, she saw a great deal of her Italian-born grandparents, who always spoke Italian and who participated in a lively household activity including music.[14] Her mother was content to remain a housewife, while her father became a local elementary school principal who started an after school program that featured dance, an art form that completely hooked four-year-old Patti. Although her father wanted her to become a teacher, her direction changed after her parents divorced, allowing Patti to pursue her dream of becoming a stage actress. Her aspirations were reflected in her participation in musical plays during junior high school, further evidenced in the song-and-dance trio she and twin brothers created, and shown even more strongly during her teenage years, as she simultaneously attended Northport High School and Julliard's Preparatory-School Division, to which she had won a scholarship. Patti then attended the Drama Division of the famed Julliard School and, despite obstacles that might have discouraged others, began to act professionally with The Acting Company, a nationally-touring, repertory-drama company in which she gave performances in many plays, including *The Robber Bridegroom* (1975), for which she received a Tony Award nomination.

She then performed in an assortment of Broadway plays, achieving deserved acclaim for her portrayal of Eva Peron of Argentina in the musical *Evita* (1979), a stunning presentation that earned LuPone her first Tony Award, for Best Leading Actress in a Musical. Throughout the 1980s she appeared on the stage on many occasions, both in the United States and in Europe, where she received an Olivier Award in 1985. Back in the United States, she continued to play award-winning roles, as in *Sweeney Todd* (2005) for which she was nominated for a Tony Award and in *Gypsy*, which garnered the Outer Critics Circle Award, the Drama League Award, the Drama Desk Award and the Tony Award in 2009. A sedulous actress, she has crafted many recordings and appeared in the following Hollywood films: *Family Prayers* (1983), *Witness* (1985), *Driving Miss Daisy* (1989), *Summer of Sam* (1999), *The 24 Hour Woman* (1999), *State and Main* (2000), and *City By the* Sea (2002). Patti's reputation as a talented, feisty and temperamental individual was confirmed in her recent autobiography, *Patti LuPone: A Memoir,* that prompted one reviewer to comment

When an actor is described as "turbulent" or "difficult," it's typically a euphemism for "a royal pain." Patti LuPone, one of the most celebrated musical theater performers of her generation, wears her anger with a difference. The role she casts herself repeatedly in *Patti LuPone: A Memoir* is that of battling victim.

> Frowned upon by snobs who don't appreciate her Italian American vibrancy, pigeonholed by critics who refuse to accept her as both a musical and dramatic force, and exploited by money-hungry producers who want to wring her dry before discarding her, she reviews her theatrical career in the feisty, score-settling spirit of someone who's been burned once too often and has made a vow with her lawyers never to let it happen again (even though, at 61, she knows it probably will).[15]

Romantically linked to actor Kevin Kline for years, she eventually married Matt Johnson and has a son named Joshua.

Born in Bayonne, New Jersey, in 1938, Frank Langella is another example of an Italian American actor who, while he has made his mark in the movies, appearing in dozens of films, also finds the theater an abiding magnet. He is best known for his role of Dracula in the movie of the same name, and as Richard Nixon in *Frost/Nixon* (2008), turning in a sturdy and credible performance for which he received abundant praise and awards, including Nomination for Best Actor. After attending schools in New Jersey, he enrolled in Syracuse University, from which he graduated with a Bachelor of Arts degree. He then began a career as a stage actor in plays like *A Cry of Players* (1968), playing opposite Anne Bancroft, *Seascape* (1975)—which earned him a Tony Award, as did his acting in *Fortune's Fool* (2002)—and in the play *Frost/Nixon* (2007). He received such rare praise for the latter that a *New York Times* critic cited Langella's titanic "portrayal of Nixon is one of those made-for-the-stage studies in controlled excess in which larger-than-life seems truer-to-life than merely life-size ever could."[16]

F. (Fahrid) Murray Abraham, who is of Syrian ancestry via his father and Italian ancestry via his mother, was born in Pittsburgh, in 1939, and grew up in Texas near the Mexican border. Using the initial F. instead of Fahrid for fear of being relegated to minor roles, Abraham achieved national acclaim and won the Academy Award for Best Actor for his compelling and convincing role as Antonio Salieri in *Amadeus* (1984), and has also appeared in a number of other movies. Notwithstanding the fact that the film vaulted him from obscurity to stardom, for a time Abraham taught theater at Brooklyn College. However, he is constantly drawn to the theater, where he has focused on Shakespearean plays and has given notable performances in *Waiting For Godot*, *Twelfth Night*, and *The Merchant of Venice*. He has appeared in Samuel Beckett plays as well as works by Gilbert and Sullivan. His theater work has earned him Drama Desk Award nominations for Best Actor in a Play, both for *Teibele and Her Demon* (1980) and for *A Life in the Theater* (1992). A family man, he is married and lives with his wife and two children in Brooklyn, New York.

The son of a bus driver, Bronx-born (in 1951) Calogero Lorenzo "Chazz" Palminteri has had an upward journey in the acting field that propelled him to a high level of accomplishment not only as an actor, but also as a writer, director and producer. But success has its price—namely two decades trying to earn tuition money for acting classes and to earn a living on the fringes of show business as a bouncer and doorman. During his early years, Chazz performed as a singer in night clubs, acted in off-Broadway theater, including in an Edward Albee play, and appeared in insignificant television roles. The occasion of his big break came when he performed in a play for which he wrote the script: *A Bronx Tale*, a one-man show premiering in 1988, in which his credible acting resulted in rave reviews from critics and enthusiastic support from theatergoers.

A Bronx Tale attracted the attention of Robert De Niro, who was instrumental in making it into a Hollywood movie in which both De Niro and Palminteri had key acting roles. The play also served to open doors to leading parts in major films such as *Bullets Over Broadway* (1994) which rewarded Chazz with an Oscar nomination for Best Supporting Actor. Befitting his big, burly physique, Palminteri was usually cast as a heavy in moving pictures, but he continued to write plays that were made into movies, including *Faithful* (1996). Keeping busy as a screenwriter and actor, Palminteri continues his stage work, notably reprising his semi-autobiographical play, *A Bronx Tale*. A significant aspect of his riveting performance is that of the gravelly-voiced storyteller intuitively playing eighteen different roles as a paean to honest Italian American workers earning a living in a tough neighborhood. In this regard, the story he tells is so convincing that it has received due acknowledgement from Italian American organizations. He has also lent his person to support Italian American fundraising activities, such as agreeing to march on Columbus Day in Providence, Rhode Island's historic Federal Hill enclave. Married to actress Gianna Ranaudo, whom he first saw in church in California, Palminteri has two children with his wife and he remains a faithful Roman Catholic. He also is a fierce New York Yankees fan whose voice occasionally is heard on a sports radio station.[17]

Born of parents of Italian descent in Chicago, Illinois in 1947, Joseph Anthony "Joe" Mantegna, Jr. has acquired a well-deserved reputation as an outstanding actor for his movie and television roles. The veteran actor, who has also worked as a producer, writer and director, was raised a Catholic, attended elementary and secondary schools in Cicero, Illinois and graduated with a degree in acting from Depaul University's Goodman School of Drama, while also playing with local bands. He began acting on the stage in 1969 in the musical *Hair* and followed with other theater appearances that culminated in high praise for his role in *Glengarry Glen Ross*, a 1982 David Mamet play that depicts repugnant subterfuges used by desperate Chicago real estate agents who engage in unprincipled practices to make sales. Joe won a Tony Award for his outstanding presentation. He has acted in other plays written by Mamet, such as *A Life in the Theater* and *Lakeboat*, thereby attesting to the strong bond between the actor and the playwright, one that prompted the observation that, "Mantegna has long served as David Mamet's alter ego both on stage and on screen."[18] Mantegna has also written, and appeared in the stage production of, *Bleacher Bums*, a recollection of the many days he spent at Wrigley Field watching the Chicago Cubs Baseball Team, which made such an impact in a televised showing that it earned an Emmy Award. Joe Mantegna is married to Arlene and they are the parents of two daughters, one of whom is Mia, who is autistic. Arlene owns and operates a Chicago–themed restaurant in California, while Joe is engaged in charitable work to aid children with autism. In addition, Mantegna has played a major part in honoring the American military by appearing at The National Memorial Day Concert.[19] In 2004, the Los Angeles Italian Film Festival honored him with a lifetime achievement award, while Hollywood honored him with a star on the Hollywood Walk of Fame.

One of three children, actor Vincent D'Onofrio, whose father worked as a theater production assistant while his mother was employed as a restaurant manager, was born in 1959 in an Italian neighborhood in Bensonhurst, Brooklyn, New York but was raised in other locations. He has become one of the most versatile and highly regarded actors of his time, employing his talents in movies and television, where he is a perennial favorite on *Law and Order: Criminal Intent,* and has also tried his hand at producing and directing. He has, in addition, performed on the stage, beginning with minor roles until he became a student of the Actors Studio and the American Stanislavsky Theatre, where he appeared in several of its plays, including *Of Mice and Men* and *Sexual Perversity in Chicago*, while, initially augmenting his income working as bouncer. This early experience convinced Vincent that acting and theater would be the career paths which would motivate him, his dedication led to his debut Broadway stage performance in 1984 in *Open Admissions*, a play that was praised by critics despite its limited run. He continued to appear in plays that have not always succeeded, such as in 1996 when he undertook the lead role in *Tooth of Crime*, a Sam Shepard work that left critics underwhelmed.[20] D'Onofrio has been married and divorced twice and is the father of a daughter and two sons. He collaborates with his sister Elizabeth D'Onofrio, who is a leading acting instructor.

John Turturro is rightly respected for his professionalism, not only as an actor who is eminently credible in a myriad of ethnic roles, but also as a writer and producer of independent films. He has likewise excelled on the stage. Turturro was born in 1957 in Brooklyn, New York, the son of a father who was a carpenter and construction worker, and a mother who was a singer in a jazz band that included her brothers. The Turturro family moved to Queens, New York where, exposed to tales of his family's Sicilian roots and his mother's singing, John exhibited a strong interest in movies and delighted in impersonations of his favorite actors. He attended local schools, where he wrote skits for neighborhood parties, and then attended the State University of New York at New Paltz, earned an Master of Fine Arts degree from the Yale School of Drama, and in 1980, while landing bit parts in movies, began a career as a stage actor in regional and off-Broadway plays. While waiting to make his breakthrough as an actor, Turturro worked in the construction field with his father, as a bartender, and even did a stint as a history teacher. He achieved a degree of success for his work in the title role in *Danny and the Deep Blue Sea* (1983), for which he won an OBIE Award for Best Performance in 1984, and followed that with his Broadway debut in *Death of a Salesman* (1984). His performance in the key role of Estragon in *Waiting for Godot* (1998) was so impressive it prompted one critic to remark: "his simplicity is the most rewarding aspect of this *Godot*."[21]

Nurtured on a diet of colorful and preposterous tales and fables narrated by his parents, John Turturro has acquired so genuine a passion for his ancestral past that it is a deep influence on his theatrical activities. Thus, in 2010, Turturro, returning once again to the theater, undertook a new play, *Fiabe Italiane,* essentially an adaptation of Italo Calvino's *Italian Folk Tales,* which achieved notable success in a tour of Italian cities and in which he also acted, along with other family members, including his son Diego and his cousin Aida Turturro.[22] John is married to actress Katherine Borowitz, with whom he has two sons.

Lauren Ambrose was born Lauren Anne D'Ambruoso, in Connecticut in 1978. Her father, Frank, a caterer, is of Italian descent while her mother, Anne, an interior decorator, is of Swedish heritage. A restive girl, Lauren attended schools in Connecticut, including the prestigious Choate Rosemary Hall, which she left to attend a magnet school in order to concentrate on acting. She spent her summers auditioning for Broadway plays and frequently worked for no money. "I was just an antsy kid, and I wanted to be an actress and I felt tortured,"[23] was the way she put it. Exhibiting a talent for acting and singing at an early age, redheaded Lauren combined an interest in theater with an interest in music—she is actually classically trained as an opera singer and has appeared in choruses in a professional opera production and with a ragtime/jazz band. She has made appearances in the dark television-comedy series *Six Feet Under*, for which she was twice nominated, in 2001 and 2002, for a Best Actress in a Supporting Role Emmy Award for her role as the ephemeral Claire. She has also appeared in a number of films, including *Can't Hardly Wait* (1998), *Psycho Beach Party* (2000), *Diggers* (2006), *Starting Out in the Evening* (2007), and *Loving Leah* (2009). Ambrose is married to professional photographer Sam Handel, with whom she has a son.

As successful as she has been in film and television, Lauren Ambrose, not surprisingly, continually returns to the stage, a medium with which she is familiar because she has been a working theater actress since she was thirteen. Ambrose's theatrical experience embraces her 2007 Broadway debut in Clifford Odets *Awake and Sing* and her performance at age twenty-eight playing the role of fourteen-year-old Juliet in a unique Shakespeare in the Park production of *Romeo and Juliet* set against a background of water. Ironically, her portrayal of Juliet, considered one of the quintessential roles of tempestuous adolescent anxiety, occurred only a few months after she gave birth to her first child, whom she breast-fed between rehearsals and acts. Her performance was so convincing that it induced once critic to write:

I'm glad to report that Lauren Ambrose achieves an acting miracle with her wonderful and touching Juliet. Best known for her Claire in the HBO drama *Six Feet Under*, Ms. Ambrose has little stage experience. But you would never know it from her accomplished, riveting performance. She doesn't play the famous 14-year-old demurely least of all is she self-consciously girlish. I was unprepared for her intelligent Juliet, though only a mature woman—Ms. Ambrose is approaching 30—can play a Juliet who becomes a woman overnight. *Romeo and Juliet* is a tragedy of love in which the impetuous lovers meet, marry and die within five days! The play hurtles toward its inevitable suicidal conclusion, and Ms. Ambrose seizes the lightning from the start.[24]

A list of other Italian American actors who acted on stage as well as screen should include Alan Alda, Danny Aiello, Tony Danza, Joseph Bologna, Charlie Pecorara, Linda Cardellini, Brenda Vaccaro, Bobby Cannavale, Michael Rispoli, and Beverly D'Angelo.

ENDNOTES

1. LindAnn Lo Schiavo, "Rafaela Ottiano: The Venetian who Played the Villainess," L'idea: On-Line Version, March, 2007, http://www.lideamagazine.com/rafaelaottiano.htm.
2. William Holtzman, Seesaw: A Dual Biography of Anne Bancroft and Mel Brooks (New York: Doubleday, 1979), 16
3. *New York Times*, November 15, 1998.
4. See Holtzman, *Seesaw:* 181–183 for enthusiastic reaction to her performance.
5. Fonda, Henry and Howard Teichmann, *Fonda: My Life* (New York: Signet Books, 1982), 20.
6. Helen Dudar: Philip Bosco: An Actor For All Seasons, *New York Times*, January 4, 1987.
7. Susan King, Los Angeles Times, November 15, 2007.
8. Mel Gussow, "Character Actors Are Taking a Star Turn," *New York Times*, May 18, 1990.
9. Critics who disapproved of his performance in "Hizzoner," nevertheless praised LoBianco for his acting in naturalist roles as in his performance in "A View From The Bridge." See *New York Times*, February 24, 1989; and *Philadelphia Inquirer*, February 24, 1989.
10. Lawrence Grobel, *The Unauthorized Biography of Al Pacino* (Leiscester: Charnwood, 2006), 10.
11. Grobel, *Pacino*, 104
12. Grobel, *Pacino*, 32
13. Jesse Green, "Her Stage Mother, Herself," *New York Times*, April 27, 2003.
14. Patti Lupone and Digby Diehl, *Patti LuPone: A Memoir* (New York: Crown Archetype, 2010), 11).
15. Charles McNulty, *Los Angeles Times*, October 10, 2010.
16. Charles McGrath, "So Nixonian That His Nose Seems to Evolve," *New York Times*, April 23, 2007.
17. Andy Dougan, *Untouchable: A Biography of Robert De Niro* (New York, Da Capo Press, 2003), 251–261.
18. Frank Sanello, "Casting Change,"*Chicago Tribune*, October 6, 1991.
19. *Washington Post*, May 5, 2007.

20. Ben Brantley, "A Clash of Rock Stars In an Existential Mode," *New York Times*, December 24, 1996.
21. Eddie Robson, *Coen Brothers* (London: Virgin Books, 2007). This work contains much material regarding the respect these producers have for Turturro's acting ability. See also *New York Times*, November 19, 1998.
22. *New York Times*, March 2, 2010.
23. New York Observer, January 3, 2002.
24. John Heilpern, *New York Observer*, June 26, 2006.

CHAPTER 3

SYMBIOTIC INTERACTION

TELEVISION AND FILM

Arguably, television has exposed more actors to American viewers than
any other visual medium. Although the ability to employ a combination of optical, mechanical and electronic technologies to transmit images
became a reality in the 1920s, it was in the 1940s and 1950s that television
truly began to emerge as a universal means of communication: whereas
172,000 American households had television sets in 1948, the number had
risen to 15.3 million in 1952 and would grow exponentially in succeeding
years, so that by the end of the twentieth century the appliance could be
found in nearly every American residence.[1] Television is a unique medium
that brings into peoples' homes an assortment of programs, ranging from
hard news and opinions to games, sports events, situation comedies,
serious drama, and made-for-television movies, among other fare. Given
the technical limitations of early television offerings and the sparseness of
quality programs in the early 1940s, critics called it a wasteland, thereby
fostering the impression that the medium posed little threat to traditional
Hollywood film production. "In the early sixties TV was always a second
choice for actors because many people thought it put a real damper on
an actor's chances in the motion picture industry," was the typical assess-
ment and indeed many Hollywood stars deliberately chose not to appear

in television shows for fear of tarnishing their film image.[2] It proved to be a short-lived reprieve, however, because television significantly improved its offerings and successfully brought major changes in cultural and social habits, becoming central to the demise of the golden age of moviedom in the process and increasingly leaving formerly-reluctant veteran actors and aspirants alike to advance their careers in television.

Although an untold number of Italian Americans actors either saw their careers start on television, or reached a level of fame on television that surpassed their Hollywood experience, only a few will be discussed as examples. Johnny Berardino has a rare distinction as being the only Hollywood actor to have earned both a World Series ring and the honor of a star in the Hollywood Walk of Fame. He was born Giovanni Berardino to immigrant parents from Bari, Ignazio and Ann Mussaco in Los Angeles, California. In school, while excelling in athletics, he also began a brief career as a child actor, appearing in some episodes of *Our Gang* and a movie venture produced by his father that was a financial failure.

John attended the University of Southern California, where he opted to play baseball instead of football, thus launching a long career as an infielder in the national pastime as a member of the St. Louis Browns, the Pittsburgh Pirates and the Cleveland Indians; as a member of the latter team that won the World Series in 1948. An accomplished all-around utility player rather than an established star, he sustained his share of injuries, which led to his decision to leave baseball and devote himself exclusively to acting, appearing in small roles in films like *Suddenly* (1954), *Them* (1954), *The Kid From Cleveland* (1949), *The Naked and the Dead* (1958) and *Seven Thieves* (1960). However, it would be the television medium that propelled him to new heights in the profession, becoming a familiar face to viewers as a special agent in the television series *I Led Three Lives* and in a variety of diverse roles in vehicles like *The Cisco Kid* and *The New Breed*. In 1963, he signed on to play the understanding Dr. Steve Hardy in *General Hospital*, the longest-running daytime soap opera series; it was the role he played until his death at age seventy-nine in 1996.[3]

Another excellent illustration of a veteran actor who has performed on stage and appeared on screen dozens of times, yet is best known for his television work, is Paul Picerni. Claiming ancestry from an Italian nobleman on his father's side, Horace Paul Picerni was born in 1922 in the Italian neighborhood of Corona, Queens, in New York. His mother Nicoletta was of Italian ancestry, as was his immigrant father, who was raised in the region of Naples and who upon coming to this country worked as a water-meter reader for New York City.[4] As the oldest of five children, Paul grew up in a distinctly Italian neighborhood, where be became such an outstanding student that he was designated class valedictorian. As a youngster, he had his mind set on becoming an attorney until he experienced the thrill of acting in an eighth-grade play, one that induced the school principal to suggest that he think about an acting career; he also encouraged young Paul to perform in stage plays throughout his remaining school years. During World War II, Paul served as a bombardier lieutenant, flew twenty-five combat missions, and was awarded the Distinguished Flying Cross. On one bombing flight, his sortie destroyed a bridge on the Kwai River–the bridge that later became the basis for a distinguished Oscar-winning movie.

Paul moved to California where he graduated from Loyola Marymount University in Los Angeles with a major in drama and thereupon became a professional actor and signed a contract with Warner Brothers. He appeared in many films, including *Breakthrough* (1950), *The Tanks Are Coming* (1951), and *Mara Maru* (1952), and also had supporting roles in dozens of other films. For thirty years he also served as half-time master of ceremonies for the Los Angeles Rams professional football team. However, he is best known for his four-year run as a federal agent on the popular TV series *The Untouchables*. The slam-bang crime drama, loosely based on the career of Prohibition-era agent Elliot Ness, starred Robert Stack, with Paul Picerni as his stocky jet-black haired, handpicked,

down-to-earth, right-hand man. One of the most famous of all television
crime dramas, it ran from 1959 to 1963 and became a prototype for similar
television shows. Picerni also appeared in the following popular television shows; *Kojak*, *Mannix*, *Gunsmoke*, *Adam-12*, *Hawaii Five-O*, *Perry
Mason*, *Rawhide*, *Bonanza*, *Zorro*, and *The Millionaire*. In succeeding
decades, Paul continued his roles both in Hollywood films and television.
He married Marie Mason in 1947, and became the father of eight children
and ten grandchildren. He was also known for his generosity in benefit
functions for Italian and Catholic causes. He was survived by his wife of
sixty-four years, along with six children, ten grandchildren and four great-
grandchildren when he passed away in 2011 at age eighty-nine.

Brooklyn-born in 1928, Vincent Edwards, the son of Italian immigrants
Vincenzo Zoino, a bricklayer, and Julia Zoino, was a twin and one of seven
children. Vincent excelled in swimming and won an athletic scholarship
to Ohio State University where he became part of the college's National
Championship team. When an appendectomy frustrated his dream of
entering the Olympics, he began studies at the American Academy of
Dramatic Arts, became a professional actor and appeared in major roles
in a few films including *The Killing* (1956). Thanks to a friendship
he developed with Mario Lanza, he was also given a part in *Serenade*
(1956). However, it was only when he appeared in *Ben Casey*, the highly
popular television series owned by a Bing Crosby production company
that he achieved a real level of stardom with a considerable following.[5]
His persona as dashing, brooding neurosurgeon Ben Casey highlighted
one of the early medical dramas that ran from 1961 to 1966 and thus
established a theme that has enduring television appeal and continues to
flourish. Exploiting his huge popularity, he released several successful
music albums in which he was featured as singer. Edwards was then able
to return to Hollywood where he played leading roles in films such as *The
Devil's Brigade* (1968). Throughout the rest of his career, he continued to
act in films and made guest appearances on television shows, while also
trying his hand at directing, without achieving, however, the popularity
of his television series. Edwards was married four times, had three chil-

dren, died in 1996 and was buried in Holy Cross Cemetery in Culver City, California.

Tony Danza, whose birth name, in 1950, was Anthony Salvatore Iadanza, became another Brooklyn-born actor whose fame is associated with television. His Sicilian-born mother, Anne Cammisa (1925-1993), and his father, Matty Iadanza (1920-1983), moved to Malverne, Long Island, where Tony attended Malverne High School. Winning a wrestling scholarship, he enrolled in and graduated from the University of Dubuque, Iowa and followed college with a professional boxing career from 1976 to 1979, amassing a nine and three record. Although he never formally studied acting, his athletic background attracted the attention of a producer who signed him to a part on the television show *Taxi*. From 1978–1983 he starred in that series as a cab-driver/boxer character named Tony. He followed this with roles on other television comedies, including *Who's The Boss?* (1984–1992) in which he played the role of a single father, and other short-lived sitcoms like *Hudson Street* (1995) and *The Tony Danza Show* (1997).

Danza's television popularity led to his first Hollywood film, *The Hollywood Knights* (1980), followed by the movie *Going Ape* (1981). However, he continued acting on television, earning a nomination for an Emmy Award in 1998 for his performance in *The Practice*. He has also won plaudits for stage acting in a revival of *The Iceman Cometh*, and in *The Producers*. In recent years, he has plumbed deeply into his ethnic background, appearing at the Clarksburg, West Virginia Italian Heritage Festival where he told stories from his childhood, tap danced, played the trumpet and piano, told jokes and sang songs. He has coauthored Tony Danza's *Father-Son Cookbook* with his son Marc, which features his family's Italian heritage in the form of recipes. He also worked as a teacher in an urban Philadelphia high school in the 2009–2010 academic year.[6] Danza has been married twice and is the father of four children.

In Yvonne DeCarlo we have another excellent example of an Italian American actress whose fame spanned both Hollywood films and television. Born in 1922 in Canada as Margaret Yvonne Middleton, the daughter of Marie De Carlo and car salesman William Middleton, who abandoned the family while she was a child, Yvonne took on the name of her Sicilian grandfather, De Carlo, when she became an actress. Under her mother's guidance, Yvonne was taken to Hollywood to enroll in dancing school. However, earning a livelihood in that field proved to be difficult for the next few years. She landed a minor role in a B movie, but continued to work in Hollywood chorus lines until she obtained major roles in Hollywood films, such as the title role in *Salome: Where She Danced* (1945), *Criss Cross* (1949), *Captain's Paradise* (1953), *The Ten Commandments* (1956), and *Band of Angels* (1957).

Unfortunately, by the early 1960s as her movie career was in serious decline; she suffered from depression, and was experiencing financial problems. However, in 1964 she turned to television, playing the female lead in *The Munsters*, a series that introduced her to a new generation of viewers. "It meant security. It gave me a new, young audience I wouldn't have had otherwise. It made me 'hot' again, which I wasn't for a while."[7] Although *The Munsters* was short lived, it became a cult sitcom that aired on reruns for years and she continued to act in both film and television. Yvonne, who became a naturalized United States citizen, was married for nineteen years to stuntman Robert Morgan, had two sons, one of whom predeceased her. She passed away in 2007 at age eighty-four.

Currently a highly successful movie producer, director and actor, Danny DeVito owes much of his fame to television. Born in Neptune, New Jersey in 1944, the son of Julia and Daniel (a small businessman), Danny, one of five children, attended Catholic grammar school and high school before enrolling in the American Academy of Dramatic Arts. His Italian American upbringing influenced him throughout his life in many ways, from his over-protectiveness regarding his children to his penchant for cigar smoking —like many an Italian immigrant of that era his father was an inveterate smoker of DiNobili cigars, known on the street as Guinea Stinkers. Determined to become an actor, Danny moved to Los Angeles,

California in 1966 but found few acting jobs because of his diminu-
tive stature (five feet tall), however, he persisted by using his camera to
shoot short documentary films and soon found bit parts in stage plays,
including a stage production of *One Flew Over the Cuckoo's Nest*. This
was the background to his appearance in movies ,commencing with a
reprisal of his memorable part in the award-winning *One Flew Over the
Cuckoo's Nest* (1975). But his fortuitous casting in the television series
Taxi (1978–1983), playing the role of Louie De Palma, a sleazy and tyran-
nical dispatcher, propelled him to a list of the fifty greatest television characters of all time. Since then, De Vito has continued his multiple roles as
actor, director, producer, and screenwriter for both feature films and television shows. Among the movies he has directed are *Throw Momma From
the Train* (1987) *The War of the Roses* (1989) and *Hoffa* (1992). He and his
wife, actress Rhea Pearlman, also own Jersey Films, which has produced
a number of highly regarded films, including *Pulp Fiction* (1994). Danny
and Rhea are the parents of three children.[8]

Born in Englewood, New Jersey, in 1954 to Helen Burke, a mother
of Irish descent and Salvatore, a father of Italian ancestry, John Joseph
Travolta was the youngest of the six children of a hard-working, middle-
class family. Because his mother, Helen, had an abiding interest in acting
—she had studied drama at Columbia University and also taught acting in
town—impersonations and imitating actors were parts of the household
interplay that particularly influenced John at a young age.[9] After a few
years at Catholic grade school and public school John attended the local
high school. However, the pull of theater caused him to leave high school
before graduation. Strongly encouraged by his parents, self-assured and
possessed of natural acting abilities, the teenage John's appearance in local
theater shows led to a contract with a personal manager, Bob Le Mond,
who molded his career by steering him toward television commercials and
guest shots intermixed with acting in stage plays and musicals, such as
Grease and *Bus Stop*.

John's television breakthrough came in 1975 when he signed on to play the role of Vinnie Barbarino, a carefree, captivating character on the sitcom *Welcome Back, Kotter*. Travolta's portrayal of a stereotypical, not-so-bright Italian American, the student leader of a slow-witted group of Brooklyn "sweathogs" caught on with the public, thereby rendering him an actor with a future. A handsome young six-footer with a shock of dark hair and blue eyes, he would go on to movie fame in films like *Saturday Night Fever* (1977), where he again played a young Italian American from Brooklyn. His character was a young man with a dead-end job who only came to life as the disco king at Saturday night dances, a role which won him a Best Actor Oscar nomination at the young age of twenty-four. He was also featured in the movie *Grease* (1978) while continuing to play in the *Welcome Back, Kotter* series.[10] After several years of unrewarding filmmaking, Travolta moved away from his early film persona to play more villainous roles, such as mobster Vincent Vega in *Pulp Fiction* (1994) for which he was once again nominated for a Best Actor Academy Award, a nomination that effectively revived his career. John, who was raised as a Roman Catholic, has become a practitioner of Scientology, is married to actress Kelly Preston and is the father of three children, one of whom, Jeff, died in 2009.

David Caruso is another Italian American actor whose fame rests largely on his television career. Having a mother of Irish descent and a father of Italian heritage, David was born in 1956 in Queens, New York, and attended Our Lady Queen of Martyrs Catholic School and Archbishop Molloy High School. Starting in 1980, he appeared in supporting roles in several films, including *An Officer and a Gentleman* (1982). In 1993 Caruso was given a featured role as Detective John Kelly on the hit television series *NYPD Blue,* which earned him a Golden Globe Award and a TV Guide citation as one of six new stars to watch in the 1993–94 season. After a few performances in the second season of the series, he once again began to pursue a film career in Hollywood, meeting, however, with limited success which compelled a return to television. He starred in *Michael Hayes*, a drama series that ran for a year. Beginning in 2002, however, he has starred as Lt. Horatio Caine in *CSI: Miami*, enjoying such a triumph that a six-inch-tall Bobble Head doll of Caruso's character, replete with sun glasses and red hair has become a popular item among his fans. Caruso has been married twice and has three children.[11]

Actress Valerie Bertinelli has been in the acting profession for some thirty-five years, most of which have been in television. The daughter of an Irish American mother and a father of Italian heritage, she was born in 1960 in Wilmington, Delaware. When the family moved to Los Angeles, Valerie studied acting and at age fifteen landed an acting role in the television series *One Day at a Time*. The long-running sitcom revolved around Ann Romano, a divorced mother, and her two teenaged daughters, one of whom was played by Bertinelli. Valerie remained with the show throughout its nine-year duration, from 1975 to 1984, appearing in 207 of its 209 shows. Following the termination of the show, Bertinelli made several made-for-TV movies and mini-series and spent time working in sitcoms, including two years in the cast of *Touched By An Angel*. She has appeared in a couple of Hollywood movies but her forte continues to be television. Throughout her career she has struggled with weight problems and has become an activist for weight loss; a passion that led to the publication of an autobiography on the subject. Her latest television show is the currently-popular *Hot in Cleveland,* with Betty White. Married once, Bertinelli was divorced and has one son.[12]

Frank Sinatra, Dean Martin and Perry Como represented a triumvirate of Italian American entertainers and children of the major Italian immigration era whose careers encompassed recording popular songs, making movies, stage singing performances and television. Called perhaps the greatest American entertainer of the twentieth century, Sinatra had achieved colossal stardom by the early 1940s. The only child of Italian immigrant parents (mother Natalie Della, father Antonio Martino Sinatra) he was born in Hoboken, New Jersey in 1915. Not inclined to formal schooling, he quit high school and took odd jobs until he began a singing career and hit pay dirt by becoming the featured vocalist for popular bands like those of Harry James and Tommy Dorsey. In time, he would have a towering movie career, including winning an 1954 Oscar for Best Supporting Actor in *From Here to Eternity* (1954), alongside his spectacular singing career. He entered the world of television in 1950, a low point in his career, with a program called *The Frank Sinatra Show*, which, critical acclaim notwithstanding, lasted only two years. In the late 1950s, Sinatra starred in a second show of similar type that continued until 1960. Thereafter, he appeared periodically in special shows that featured his singing and that won him an Emmy Award for *Frank Sinatra, A Man and His Music* (1965).

Sinatra's Hollywood career was also legendary. It included singing "I Fall in Love Too Easily" in *Anchors Aweigh* (1945), which was nominated for the Academy Award for Best Original Song; winning the Best Supporting Actor Award in *From Here to Eternity* (1953); earning a nomination for the Best Actor Award for his role in *The Man With the Golden Arm*, (1954); singing "All the Way" in *Pal Joey* (1957), which won the Academy Award for Best Song; singing "High Hopes," which won the Best Original Song Award, in *A Hole in the Head* (1959), a film he also produced; and garnering an Academy Award nomination for Best Original Song for "My Kind of Town," in *Robin and the 7 Hoods* (1964). That Frank Sinatra was one of stage, screen and television's greatest actors is a given. If nothing else, his Oscar-winning film performances, his efforts at directing (*None But the Brave,* 1965) and producing (*A Hole in the Head* 1959), and his outstanding television and singing careers speak to his astonishing versatility and range. Sinatra had three children with his first wife, Nancy Barbato, and was married four times altogether. A Funeral Mass was offered for him at the Roman Catholic Church of the Good Shepherd, in Beverly Hills, California at the time of his death in 1998 at age eighty-two.[13]

The son of an Italian immigrant father from Abruzzo and a mother whose Italian forbears descended from Naples and Sicily, Dean Martin (Dino Paul Crocetti) was born in Steubenville, Ohio in 1917, the younger of two sons. He spoke only the Italian language until he started school, and consequently was the target of much ridicule for his broken English. Early prognostications regarding his future were dubious. Would he become a barber like his father?[14] The early signs were unpromising but deceptive— he quit school, worked in various low-paying jobs and became a boxer— until he entered the realm of show business, becoming a fairly successful nightclub singer. He initially sang under the name Dino Martini in hopes of sharing the publicity then being enjoyed by the popular Nino Martini, an Italian singer of a similar name.[15] His fortunes really shot upwards once he teamed up with Jerry Lewis, becoming part of one of the hottest comedy shows in the business, and he began to appear in films, continuing to make a strong impression in the medium long after he went solo. Because he chose to continue making films while appearing in nightclub performances, Martin initially hesitated to enter the world of television, however, he overcame his early reluctance, and signed onto the medium, headlining a long-running television variety venue titled *The Dean Martin Show* which ran from 1965 to 1974. The popularity of the show continues into the twenty-first century in the form of huge, ongoing DVD sales. Martin was married three times and, at the time of his death in 1995 at age seventy-eight, had four surviving children. Funeral services were held in Westwood Memorial Park, California.[16]

Although Perry Como appeared in a few Hollywood movies, he never achieved the status enjoyed by Sinatra or Martin as film actors; however, he would come to surpass them both on television as he became one of the most successful television entertainers of all time. He was born in the coal-mining town of Canonsburg, Pennsylvania in 1912, the seventh son of a seventh son, and one of thirteen children. His Abruzzo-born parents were determined to provide music lessons for all their children—for Perry it meant instructions on the organ and baritone horn and playing in local Italian street bands. As a youngster, Perry (born Pierino Ronald) was intent on becoming a barber and earned a living in that trade until he began making recordings for RCA. As his popularity rose, people bought his records in large quantities—eventually he would sell over one hundred million platters—a sum that attested to his immense stature in the field. He sang on radio shows and in 1950 entered the field of television by hosting his own program, first for CBS and then for NBC. He was considered a pioneer in the television-variety-show genre in which, wearing a cardigan sweater, he practiced his trademark, relaxed, low-keyed, casual singing style that would be emulated by many others. *Perry Como's Kraft Music Hall,* originally called *The Perry Como Show,* was a long-running (1948–1966) TV series, which won five Emmy Awards for excellence in television.[17] In later years, his Christmas specials on ABC became woven into the fabric of the popular culture of the time. Perry Como was married once, to Roselle, a marriage that lasted sixty-five years and produced three children. He was eighty-eight years old at the time of his death in 2001. A funeral Mass for him was held in St. Edward's Catholic Church, Palm Beach, Florida.[18] Years later, the town of his birth, in an attempt to boost tourism, erected a life-sized statue of the crooner and played his greatest hits for hours.[19]

The award-winning HBO series *The Sopranos* (1999–2007) has been the television vehicle that brought acclaim to several actors of Italian American ancestry, among them James Gandolfini, Edie Falco and Michael Imperioli. James Gandolfini's mother was brought up in Italy, as was his father, who became a bricklayer and then head custodian at Paramus Catholic High School, New Jersey. Born in Westwood, New Jersey in 1961, James was molded by his parents, who spoke Italian at home and provided the nourishing atmosphere of a devout Catholic family. Armed with a degree from Rutgers University, James entered the acting field, appearing on stage and in film. It is his role as the Mafia boss in *The Sopranos*, which earned him three Emmy Awards for Best Actor in a Drama, for which he is best known.

Edie Falco's mother is of Swedish background, while her father has Italian ancestry. Edie was born in Brooklyn and grew up in Long Island, graduating from Northport High School. A graduate of SUNY Purchase, Edie began to act and appeared in various television shows and films,

some of which have led to awards. Her role as Carmela Soprano, a sympathetic but sad woman, who is both repelled by her husband's activities and
yet remains loyal to him, has won many awards.[20]

(James) Michael Imperioli, born in Mount Vernon, New York in 1966,
is the son of Dan Imperioli, a bus driver who is also an amateur actor. He
graduated from Sacred Heart High School in Yonkers, New York, attended
St. Catherine's in Ringwood, New Jersey and studied acting at New York
City's Stella Adler Conservatory. Michael has appeared in many films,
usually typecast as a New York Italian mobster, commencing with his
first Hollywood acting role, in the 1990 Academy Award-winning movie
Goodfellas, in which he played a local kid who does errands for gang-
sters. He also had roles in *Jungle Fever* (1991) *Malcom X* (1992) and
Clockers (1995). However, he is better known for his television acting
career, including his part as a low-ranking soldier in the Soprano gangster family, for which he won a Primetime Emmy Award for Outstanding
Supporting Actor in a Drama Series in 2004, and for which he has been
nominated for a Golden Globe Award. He has also starred as a detective in
the popular television series *Law and Order* and starred in the show *Life
on Mars;* he was chosen for the part because he "is a perfect example of
an actor who exudes a New York attitude," according to Gary Newman,
cochairman of 20th Century Fox Television, which is producing the show
along with ABC Studios. "His look and his talents are perfect for this
series." There were times, however, when he acted against the gangster
stereotype, as in the movie *Lovely Bones* (2009) in which plays a benevo-
lent and compassionate cop.[21] Imperioli is active in the New York theater
scene as an actor, producer, director of plays and cofounder of a theater
company called Machine Full. In 1995 he married Victoria Chlebowski
and has three children.

Born in New York City in 1960, Melissa Leo describes her parents as
hippies—her mother Peggy taught school part time and her father Arnold
Leo was a book editor who quit his position to become a commercial
fisherman. Melissa was raised on Manhattan's Lower East Side until her

parents divorce led to economic hard times for her and her mother, who were evicted from their apartment for failure to pay rent, then moved first to a commune, and then to other locations. Never having much money, Melissa attended SUNY Purchase for a time, but dropped out and moved to New York City, where she worked as a waitress while seeking to enter the acting profession. She got her first break auditioning for Bill Murray and in 1984 began appearing in television shows such as *All My Children*. Melissa became a television fixture and female-detective role model in her role as tough homicide Detective Kay Howard in *Homicide: Life in the Streets*. Because there was no dress code for such a role, Leo, in keeping with her persona as a working-class actress, decided to appear in commonplace, unpretentious, and unadorned trousers bereft of frills and makeup. After starring in that role for years she continued to find employment in television and movie roles that brought her critical acclaim. She came in second in the race for the 2004 Los Angeles Film Critics Association Award for Best Supporting Actress for her performance in *21 Grams* (2003), won the 2008 Utah Film Critics Association Award for Best Lead Performance by an Actress for her work in *Frozen River* (2008), and in February 2011 received the Best Supporting Actress Academy Award for her role in *The Fighter*. The journeyman actress has a son but has never married.[22]

Among other actors whose popularity was due as much to television as to their Hollywood film careers was Daniel J. Travanti, (Danielo Giovanni Travanti) born to Italian immigrant parents in Wisconsin. An athlete and an outstanding student who earned scholarships to Ivy League schools, he decided to attend the University of Wisconsin-Madison instead.[23] Although he made a several Hollywood movies, he is best-known for his starring role as Captain Frank Furillo in the television drama *Hill Street Blues* (1981–1987) for which he won an Emmy Award.

Connecticut-born Anthony Peter Musante has appeared in a number of films made in the United States and abroad, however, he became better known for his work on television series *Toma* and *As The World Turns*.

Born of Italian American working-class parents in Brooklyn, New York, Paul Sorvino took acting and singing lessons that led to an acting career on stage and in feature movies. He also gained a large following for his role as Detective George Dzundza in the popular series *Law and Order* (1991–1993). Of partial Italian descent, Florida born Shawn Caminiti Pyfrom is another actor who has appeared in several movies and television, with appearances on *Desperate Housewives* from 2005–2009. Although actress Justine Avignon Miceli, born in Sunnyside, Queens, New York in 1959, has appeared in a couple of full-length movies, such as *Dangerous Beauty* (1998) and *True Crime* (2005), most of her acting career has been spent performing for television. In preparation for her acting career she attended New York's High School for the Performing Arts and studied acting at the California Institute of the Arts. She began her professional career acting in commercials, off-Broadway shows and daytime television shows. She soon appeared in primetime venues like *Law and Order* and in 1994 became a star in the highly successful police drama *NYPD Blue*. She has since played guest roles on television as well as commercials.

Maria Bello was born in 1967 in Norristown, Pennsylvania, a Philadelphia suburb, into a blue-collar family of four children. Her father, of Italian descent, was a construction worker, while her mother, of Polish background, was a nurse. She was educated in Catholic schools, including Villanova University, where she studied political science but, after taking an acting class, switched her major to acting. "I knew that's what I should be doing," she explained. Encouraged by a priest mentor, Maria continued in her new field of theater by obtaining minor acting roles in New York City before her breakthrough on television performing in a number of venues, such as Mr. And Mrs. Smith, ER, and *Law and Order: Special Victims Unit*. Bello has also made a number of movies that have elicited positive reviews from critics.[24] Her leading role in *The Cooler* (2003) and her portrayal of the stricken wife caught up in a swirl of aggression in *A History of Violence* (2005) brought her Golden Globe nominations for Best Supporting Actress. She continues to work as an actress for television, and is slated to play a female detective in a new series, *Prime Suspect*. Maria has a son and is unmarried.[25]

ENDNOTES

1. James T. Patterson, *Grand Expectations, The United States, 1915–1974* (: Oxford University Press, 1996), 348.
2. Ben Gazzara, *In The Moment, My Life As An Actor* (New York: Carroll and Graf, 2004), 129.
3. Otto Bruno, "Legends," *Fra Noi,* March, 2011.
4. Paul Picerni with Tom Weaver, *Steps to Stardom: My Story* (Duncan, Oklahoma: BearManor Media, 2007), 1–12.
5. Armando Cesari, *Mario Lanza: An American Tragedy* (Fort Worth, Texas: Baskerville Publishers, 2004), 207.
6. *Washington Post*, October 1, 2010.
7. *Los Angeles Times*. January 11, 2007.
8. David Shaw, "DeVito," *Cigar Aficionado*, Dec 1 1996, 1–7.
9. Kathleen Brady, *John Travolta, A Biography,* People Profiles (Bishop Books, 2000), 13–15.
10. See Margherita Heyer–Caput, "Italian American urban Hyphens in Saturday Night Fever, *Italian Americana* 24, no. 1 (Winter 2011): 34–49 for an analysis of the film Saturday Night Fever in which bridge is used as metaphor infusing hopes of liberation and self fulfillment.
11. *Parade Magazine*, March 6, 2005.
12. Valerie Bertinelli, Losing it: And Gaining My Life Back One Pound at a Time (Nw York: Free Press, 2008).
13. Pete Hamill, *Why Sinatra Matters* (Boston: Little, Brown, 1999); Stanislao G. Pugliese, *Frank Sinatra: History, Identity and Italian American Culture* (New York: Palgrave Macmillan, 2004).
14. Deanna Martin, *Memories Are Made of This: Through His Daughter's Eyes* (New York: Three Rivers Press, 2004), 8.
15. Martin, Memories Are Made of This, 10.
16. Martin, Memories Are Made of This, 253.
17. Pittsburgh Post–Gazette, December 15, 1990.
18. Salvatore Primeggia, "Comedy," in *The Italian American Experience: An Encyclopedia*, eds. Salvatore J. LaGumina et al. (New York: Routledge 1999), 130–133.
19. Richard Severo, "Perry Como, Relaxed and Elegant Troubadour of Recordings and TV, Is Dead at 88," *New York Times*, May 13, 2001.
20. Emily Nussbaum, "The Lonliest Soprano," *New York*, April 1, 2001.

21. Jeff Simon, "A good guy at last: Michael Imperioli talks about 'Lovely Bones'"*Buffalo News*, January 18, 2010.
22. Los Angeles *Italia*, February 20–26, 2011; Logan Hill, "57 Minutes With Melissa," *New York Magazine*, January 23, 2011.
23. Margherita Marchione, *Americans of Italian Heritage* (New York: University Press of America, 1995), 214–218.
24. Amy Spencer, "Full of Grace: Maria Bello," *New York Post*, July 27, 2008.
25. Jim DiStasio, "On Her Own Terms," *Fra Noi*, September 2011, 25–26.

CHAPTER 4

THE ITALIAN AMERICAN SONGBOOK

Essential to setting a mood appropriate to a script, a mood that engages the audience and that might even find exiting movie house patrons humming the refrains they had just heard, songs, melodies and jingles have been part of moviemaking from its beginning. Live pianists played tunes to accompany projections of early Silent Era films in small movie houses, while in large establishments, ensembles of musicians were sometimes part of the entertainment. Alternatively, premier movie emporiums housed giant organs equipped with a wide range of special features that supplied fitting sound effects. Italian Americans have been and continue to be a considerable part of the full spectrum of music, songs, and musical biographies that are a rich part of Hollywood lore.

Perhaps the first Italian American songwriter to compose music that appeared as soundtracks or featured songs in film was Albert Joseph Piantadosi, born in 1884 in Manhattan's Italian quarter. Albert attended St. James School in New York to study medicine. However, he turned to music, where he achieved considerable success and fame sufficient to rival the young Irving Berlin. The two were indeed competitors, each playing

piano and composing songs in popular turn-of-the-century beer halls—
Piantadosi in Callahan's and Berlin in the Pelham. Reverting to his ethnic
background, one of Piantadosi's first hit songs was titled "My Mariuccia
Take a Steamboat," a song which was rendered even more entertaining
as steamboats on the East River tooted their horns at appropriate places
during the playing of the music. When the song lured customers from
Pelham's establishment, it served as a catalyst for Berlin to respond by
writing his own Italianate song, "Marie From Sunny Italy." Piantadosi
wrote many hit songs, some of which became background music during
the silent screen era, such as the title song in the film *The Woman Thou
Gavest Me* (1915). The advent of talking pictures saw his songs enriching
films, songs like; "I Didn't Raise My Boy to be a Soldier," a major paci-
fist anti-war song written in 1915 and appearing in *Ace of Aces* (1933);
"The Curse of an Aching Heart" in *Rose of Washington Square* (1939);
"Someday I'll Dream Again" in *Crazy House* (1943); and "Honey Man
My Little Lovin Honey Man" in *Wabash Avenue* (1950). Piantadosi, who
established his own music company and who was said to have introduced
ragtime to Europe, died in Encino, California in 1995, survived by his
wife.[1]

   While many Italian American songwriters provided gorgeous melodies
for Hollywood that are indelibly identified with memorable films,
undoubtedly at the head of the list is Harry Warren—he is reported to
have been the first songwriter to write music primarily for movies. He was
born in Brooklyn, New York in 1893 as Salvatore Antonio Guaragna, one
of eleven children of Italian immigrant parents. His mother was named
Rachel, while Antonio, his father, who worked as a boot maker, decided
to change the family name to Warren—Salvatore became Harry Warren.
Harry possessed an uncanny ability to sight-read music that drew him to
Our Lady of Loretto, the local Catholic Church, where he served as an
altar boy and sang in the choir. Although limited family financial resources
precluded formal music lessons, young Harry pursued his interest in music
by teaching himself to play his father's accordion and by singing in the
church choir. Impressed by his obvious musical talent, the church organist

took such a deep interest in him that she gave him musical instruction, teaching him to identify chords and scales—the only proper lessons he ever had. At an early age Harry quit school to play drums profession-ally, performing in a traveling band until 1915, when he landed a job with a silent movie company that had him carrying out a variety of jobs, including playing piano mood music for the actors as well as actually appearing in films. Harry also began to write music during the First World War after he joined the Navy—it was the beginning of a spectacular songwriting career that continued throughout his life. The output of his life's work was staggering, totaling the composition of over eight hundred songs. Since many appeared in more than one film, three hundred of these songs were eventually heard in fifty-six movies. His songs, ranging from *Looney Tunes* cartoons to movie extravaganzas, resulted in collaboration with some of the finest lyricists of the day, like Johnny Mercer, Billy Rose and Ira Gershwin. Employed by major Hollywood studios, Harry was an essential component of success as the composer of hit songs for all the studios, especially with the blockbuster musical *42nd Street* (1933), produced by Warner Brothers. His music has appeared in Hollywood films repeatedly over the years as, for instance, "Zing A Little Zong" an Oscar-nominated tune sung by Bing Crosby in *Just For You* (1952), "That's Amore" sung by Dean Martin in *The Caddy* (1953), "Innamoratta" in *Artists and Models* (1955), the title song in *An Affair To Remember* (1957), and "I Love My Baby (My Baby Loves Me)" in *Zelig* (1983). Altogether, forty-two of his songs hit the top ten of *Your Hit Parade*—more than any other composer.

It is stunningly ironic that, his gigantic productivity notwithstanding, he is not familiar to the public. Warren had more number-one songs on *Your Hit Parade* than any of his contemporaries, including Cole Porter, Irving Berlin, George Gershwin and Richard Rodgers, yet he remained hardly known. His anonymity was a source of regret. "The basic drive of my life has been my love of music, and if people have like music [*sic*] it has to be because it came from the heart. My only regret is that it hasn't brought me more personal recognition." It became still more annoying when even people in the movie business failed to recognize him. "It gets a little irksome to hear myself referred to as America's greatest unknown songwriter." [2]While it is interesting to speculate as to how deeply his ethnic background informed his writing, we unfortunately have little information on the matter. Nevertheless it must have been profound; he was quoted as having misgivings regarding his name change, confessing, "I'm sorry now that I changed it but what are you going to do about it? I tell everybody I am Italian." In his professional work, his Italian heritage was undeniable. When Bing Crosby asked who had inspired him in his musical work, Warren's response was instantaneous—Puccini. He also told popular entertainer Carmen Miranda, who complimented him on writing such good Brazilian tunes, that "They're all Italian tunes with another beat." At least a few of his song titles possess an unmistakable Italian connection: "Innamorrata," "Where Do You Worka John?," and "That's Amore." He received eleven Academy Award nominations and actually won three Oscars for the following works: "Lullaby of Broadway," the title song in the movie by the same name; "You'll Never Know" in *Hello Frisco, Hello* (1943); and "On the Atchison, Topeka and the Santa Fe," featured in *The Harvey Girls* (1942). He was married in 1917, had two children and died in 1981.[3]

Although Warren was the most prolific Italian American popular songwriter, there were many others, such as the previously mentioned Piantadosi, along with Frankie Carle, James V. Monaco, Ray Anthony, Carmen Lombardo, Henry Mancini, Phil Brito, Teddy Randazzo and Bob Gaudio, in addition to Italian nationals Nino Rota and Ennio Morricone. Italian-born (in Fornia, 1885) James Vincent Monaco—sometimes known as Ragtime Jimmy—came to Chicago with his family when he was six. A self-taught pianist, he worked as a ragtime player in Chicago's fancy Savoy Club and then moved to New York, where he was employed as a piano player in cabaret clubs, enjoying success with his song "Oh, You Circus Day," which was featured in the 1912 Broadway show *Hanky Panky*. One of his biggest hits was "You Made Me Love You" written in 1913 for the Broadway review *Honeymoon Express* and popularized by Al Jolson, later, with lyrics revised for Judy Garland, the song was featured in *Broadway Melody of 1938*. The song was recorded by many singers, such as Doris Day, and popular bands like Harry James', for which it was embellished with a fine trumpet solo. Monaco's 1927 song "Dirty Hands, Dirty Face" became the first tune sung on film by Al Jolson in *The Jazz Singer.* He also had another hit in "Row, Row, Row," which was highlighted in *The Follies of 1912.* From 1932 to 1936 he led his own dance band while simultaneously teaming up with lyricist Johnny Burke to produce songs for several Bing Crosby films, including "I've Got a Pocketful of Dreams" in *Sing You Sinners* (1938) and "Only Forever" in *Rhythm on the River* (1940) that earned a Best Song Oscar nomination for the smash hit. He received four Academy Award nominations for his tunes that were featured in movies, including "Only Forever," "I'm Making Believe," and "An Apple for the Teacher."[4] Monaco wrote songs for so many Hollywood stars, including June Haver, Martha Raye, Betty Grable and Mary Martin, that when he died in California in 1945 at age sixty, many of them were present at his memorial service—one of the biggest ever staged by Hollywood's elite. He was survived by his wife.

For more than a half a century Frankie Carle was a fixture on the music scene in America. Francis Carlone (his original name) was born in Providence, Rhode Island in 1903. Taught to play the piano by his uncle Nicholas Colangelo, the precocious piano player actually began working in his uncle's band at age thirteen earning one dollar a week.[5] By the 1920s he was playing in some of the country's top bands, where he inter-mixed with many of the most highly esteemed contemporary musicians and recorded for the first time. He started his own band in 1941 while also writing music, including his best known score, "Sunrise Seranade," (coau-thored with Jack Lawrence), which became a signature piece for Glenn Miller and which was featured in the film *The Fabulous Dorseys* (1947). Carle had several hit songs recorded by his daughter Marjorie Hughes, including: "Falling Leaves," "Lovers' Lullaby" (with Larry Wagner), "Roses in the Rain," "Sunrise in Napoli," and "Oh, What it Seemed to Be," made popular by Frank Sinatra. In 1949 his band was featured in the movie *My Dream is Yours*. He died at age ninety-seven in 2001 and was survived by his companion, a daughter, and two grandchildren.

Carmen Lombardo, whose Italian immigrant father was a tailor, was born in Canada in 1903 and was one of seven children and the younger brother of well-known bandleader Guy Lombardo. Together with three of his brothers who also played in Guy's band, he moved to the United States, where he became the lead saxophonist in his brother's durable band. He was also a vocalist and composer whose compositions included the 1928 classic "Sweethearts on Parade," "Coquette," "Boo Hoo," "Some Rainy Day," and he coauthored "Powder Your Face With Sunshine (Smile, Smile, Smile). " He wrote, with John Jacob Loeb, the words and music for Guy Lombardo's Jones Beach stage creations called the *Arabian Nights* (1954, 1955), *Paradise Island* (1961, 1962), and *Mardi Gras* (1965, 1966). A number of his works appeared in cartoon films as well as in Woody Allen movies such as *Zelig* (1983), which featured Carmen's "A Sailboat in the Moonlight." In addition, Carmen also appeared with the Guy Lombardo band in three movies: *Many Happy Returns* (1934), *Stage Door Canteen* (1943) and *No Leave, No Love* (1946). He was married and had no children at the time of his death in 1971.[6]

Although Ray Anthony (Raymond Antonini) was born in 1922 in Pennsylvania, he moved at an early age to Cleveland, Ohio with his family, where he studied trumpet with his father and played with the family band. That he was a talented musician is evident in the fact that at age eighteen (1940–1941) he was invited to play with the fabulous Glenn Miller Orchestra and appeared in the movie *Sun Valley Serenade* (1941). Following his World War II stint in the Navy, he formed his own band that became popular playing, among others, his own compositions, including "Thunderbird," "Bunny Hop," "Trumpet Boogie," "Big Band Boogie," and "Mr. Anthony's Boogie." He served as a television musical director, starred in his own variety show and acted in movies, appearing in several films during the late 1950s, such as *The Five Pennies* (1959) in which he portrayed band leader Jimmy Dorsey. Anthony and his band were also featured in the movie *The Girl Can't Help It* (1956). He was famous for his music arrangements for television shows including *Dragnet* and *Peter Gunn*, the latter composed by Henry Mancini. He continues to record band music into the twenty-first century.[7]

Although he was born in 1924 in Cleveland's Little Italy, Henry Mancini (Enrico Nicola Mancini) moved with his family to West Aliquippa, Pennsylvania where his Abruzzo-born father Quinto worked as a steelworker.[8] An only child who was sickly , Henry learned to play the flute so proficiently that it elicited the attention of the head of the Music Department at Aliquippa High School, which Henry would later attend. While his music talent opened doors for him socially when he was a teenager, he was always sensitive that his Italian background was a bar to true acceptance.[9] Henry also took piccolo and piano lessons and began to play in various venues, including a local Sons of Italy band. For a time he attended Carnegie Tech and then the famous Julliard School of Music, only to depart in order to serve in the Army during the Second World War. He was influenced by the music of Duke Ellington and, upon his return to civilian life, played in the Glenn Miller orchestra, then under the leadership of Tex Beneke. He also studied serious music until 1952, when he went to work for Universal Studios composing and arranging music for over one hundred movies, among them *The Glenn Miller Story* (1954), for which he received an Academy Award nomination. Mancini influenced the music that came to be incorporated in films in the post–World War II-era in a seminal way. Until his time, "film scoring was almost entirely derived from European symphonic composition. Mancini changed that. More than any other person, he americanized film scoring, and in time European film composers followed his path.[10] As an independent composer and arranger he scored music for television, notably the theme for the series *Peter Gunn,* and also wrote the theme music for movies such as *The Pink Panther* (1963); *Breakfast At Tiffany's* (1961), which featured his composition of the title song "Moon River" (lyrics by Johnny Mercer); and *Days of Wine and Roses* (1962). Throughout the course of his forty-year career Mancini won twenty Grammy Awards, was nominated for eighteen Academy Awards and was the winner of four such awards.

Mancini was also a concert performer, conducting world-class symphony orchestras in major international venues, including command performances for the British Royal family. Mancini's forty-three year marriage to singer Virginia "Ginny" O'Connor produced three children who, together with his wife, survived him upon his death in California at age seventy in 1994. The high regard for Mancini's contribution to American culture is reflected in United States Postal Service designation of the musician with a thirty-seven cent commemorative stamp—one of the few Italian Americans to be so honored.[11]

Although not known primarily as song writers, but rather as performers who influenced Hollywood in others ways that will be treated elsewhere in this volume, a word must be said about a couple of individuals who merit inclusion in the American songbook. One was comedian Jimmy Durante, who was deeply associated with music, even to the extent of owning the Jimmy Durante Music Publishing Company, which published dozens of his songs, some of which were performed in movies. For instance, his composition (with Jack Barnett) of "Nobody Wants My Money" was featured in *The Milkman* (1950); "She's A Little Bit This and a Little Bit That," and "I'm The Guy Who Found the Lost Chord" appeared in *This Time for Keeps* (1947); and "Did Your Ever Have That Feeling?" was in the film *New Adventures of Get Rich Quick Wallingford* (1931). Perhaps the most popular of his songs was the ditty "Inka Dinka Doo," written in 1933, which Jimmy sang in the film documentary *That's Entertainment Part II* (1976).[12]

Louis Prima was another gifted musician whose songwriting ability was impressively demonstrated by his 1936 composition of what came to be acknowledged as the iconic swing classic, "Sing, Sing, Sing." Although Prima recorded the piece with his New Orleans band, it was bandleader Benny Goodman's recording, which featured such great swing musicians as Harry James on the trumpet and Gene Krupa on the drums, that became widely popular and helped establish Goodman's King of Swing title. The song was played in the movies *The Benny Goodman Story* (1955), *All That Jazz* (1979), *Manhattan Murder Mystery* (1993), and *Leatherheads* (2008), among others. Prima also wrote the song "Sunday Kind of Love," that was played in the film *Eve's Bayou* (1997).

Phil Brito, Teddy Randazzo, and Bob Gaudio are additional songwriters of Italian descent who wrote popular ballads that gained a wide audience and who also either appeared in or provided music as the backdrop for some films. Born in West Virginia in 1915, Phil Brito (born Colombrito) enjoyed a career that encompassed composing music, writing lyrics, singing, and acting. He was one of the earliest Italian American crooners to appear in film. His is the voice singing the title song in *Come Back to Sorrento* (1943), in *The Sweetheart of Sigma Chi* (1946), and he sang the title song in *Music Man* (1948), in which he had an acting/singing role as Phil Russo. One of the songs he sang was his own composition "I Could Swear It Was You." Brito also wrote the English lyrics for the sentimental song "Mama," which had become a favorite within Italian American communities. Brito died at age ninety in 2005 in New Jersey.[13]

Brooklyn-born as Alessandro Carmelo Randazzo in 1935, Teddy Randazzo wrote hundreds of hit songs that resonated with audiences like, "It's Gonna Take a Miracle," "Hurt So Bad," and "Goin Out of My Head," that were recorded by the major singing artists of the day. "Goin Out of My Head," for example, has been recorded by over fifty artists. He was also featured in rock films such as *Hey, Let's Twist* (1961), *Mr. Rock and Roll* (1957) and *Rock, Rock, Rock* (1957). Randazzo continued writing and arranging music until his death in 2003, at age sixty-eight, leaving his wife Sheely and several children.[14]

Bob Gaudio, born in the Bronx in 1942, enjoys a highly successful musical career which has included time as a singer with the Four Seasons and as a prolific songwriter who composed hit melodies that helped the careers of many popular singers. Songs like "Sherry," "Big Girls Don't Cry," and "Can't Take My Eyes Off You," among others, helped catapult

Frankie Valli to an astounding career. Moreover, many of these songs, like "Can't Take My Eyes Off You," have been featured in films like *The Deer Hunter* (1978), *Conspiracy Theory* (1997) and *The Fabulous Baker Boys* (1989).[15] In addition, Gaudio worked as a producer and composer of the musical *Peggy Sue Got Married*, based on the popular motion picture of that name.

Several musicians of Italian ancestry have been the source of film music derived from a more traditional classical heritage. One of the more outstanding of them was Nino Rota (Giovanni Rota Rinaldi), born in 1911 into a musical family in Milan, Italy and a child prodigy—he wrote an oratorio at age eleven—who became one of the most prolific composers of film scores. The sturdiness of his musical education at the Conservatory of Santa Cecilia, and, at the suggestion of Arturo Toscanini, the Curtis Institute of Philadelphia, as well as the University of Milan, attests to his exceptional preparation and industriousness. He also taught at the Bari Conservatory. His prodigious output of serious music resulted in composing ten operas, five ballets, and dozens of orchestral, symphonic, and choral pieces. He scored music for one hundred fifty films made in Europe and the United States, including all the memorable music for Federico Fellini's films, which thereby rendered them into more unified and cohesive productions. He also composed the music for Franco Zeffirelli's Shakespeare films and the first two films of Francis Ford Coppola's *Godfather* trilogy, earning an Academy Award (shared with Carmine Coppola) for the Best Original Score in 1974. Rota, whose music was ranked near the top of the greatest film scores, died in 1979.[16]

Born in Rome in 1928, Ennio Morricone was the son of musicians and a child prodigy who wrote his first composition when he was six years old. He studied classical music in Italy's most prestigious music schools until the 1950s, when he began to earn a living as a musician, writing and playing avant-garde music even while he continued to write classical pieces. In the 1960s, Morricone began writing scores for so-called spaghetti westerns, like *The Good, the Bad and the Ugly* (1966) and *Once*

Upon a Time in the West (1968).[17] One of the most prolific composers and conductors in movie history, he is credited with over five hundred scores for television shows and films, including the scores to such memorable, award-winning movies as *The Battle of Algiers* (1966) and *Cinema Paradiso* (1988). Morricone has earned five Academy Award nominations for original scores: *Days of Heaven* (1978), *The Mission* (1986), *The Untouchables* (1987), *Bugsy* (1991), and *Malena* (2000). Although these nominations did not result in an Oscar, in 2007 the Academy Awards did extend an Honorary Oscar to Morricone "in recognition of his magnificent and multifaceted contributions to the art of film music."

Among the contemporary music composers who has made an impact in Hollywood is Michael Giacchino, born in 1967 in New Jersey, where he graduated from Holy Cross High School in Delran. He later attended the Julliard School and the School of Visual Arts in New York City. He has achieved success writing music for award-winning video games and television and in films such as *Jurassic Park* (1997) and *Rotatouille* (2007), the score for which earned him an Oscar nomination for Best Score in 2008. A higher honor came in 2010, when Giacchino won the Academy Award for the Best Original Score for the animated movie *UP*. Strongly identifying with his Abruzzi and Sicilian heritage, he has obtained Italian citizenship alongside his United States citizenship.

Another accomplished, contemporary, Hollywood music composer is Marco Beltrami, born in Long Island, New York, in 1966, of a father of Italian descent and a mother with Greek ancestry.[18] Beltrami's proficiency and versatility would make him one of the most highly-regarded composers in the field. Beginning in grade school, young Marco acquired an interest in music that was manifest in his piano playing and musical composition. His formal education included attendance at Ward Melville High School, Brown University, the Yale School of Music, the Thorton School of Music at the University of Southern California, and study under esteemed musicians in Venice, Italy. Beltrami's years of working in the field of classical music provided the background for his entry into the world of musical composition for television shows, which soon led to a job scoring the music for his first film, the thriller *Death Match* (1994). He followed this by writing the score for *The Scream* (1996), thereby further cementing his lock on the horror/thriller film genre, although he would move beyond it. Thus, after composing music for several horror films, in 2007 he earned an Academy Award nomination for his music in the remake of *3:10 to Yuma,* which won plaudits for his excellent handling of rhythm and complex musical metric patterns. In 2010 he received a second such nomination as cocomposer of the score for *The Hurt Locker,* for which critics credited him with creating music appropriate for the film that had the power to evoke feelings of fear, stress and alienation.

ENDNOTES

1. Patricia K. Hanson and Amy Dunkleberger, eds., *The American Film Institute Catalog of Motion Pictures Produced in the United States*, 2:497.
2. Tony Thomas, *Harry Warren and the Hollywood Musical* (Secaucus, New Jersey: Citadel Press, 1975), 320.
3. Mark Rotella, *Amore: The Story of the Italian American Song* (New York: Farrar, Straus and Giroux, 2010) 138, 149, 188. See also Thomas, *Harry Warren*, 1.
4. Ken Bloom and Michael Feinstein, *The American Songbook: The Singers, Songwriters & The Songs* (New York: Black Dog & Leventhal, 2005), 77, 190–192, 238.
5. Gene Catrambo, *Golden Touch: Frankie Carle* (Roslyn Heights, NY: Libra Publishers, 1980) check it out See also LaGumina et al., *Italian American Experience: An Encyclopedia*, 143.
6. Booton Herndon, *The Sweetest Music This Side of Heaven: The Guy Lombardo Story* (New York: McGraw-Hill, 1964); and Beverly Fink Cline, *The Lombardo Story* (Don Mills. Ontario:Musson, 1979).
7. *Merced Sun-Star*, Feb. 3, 1981. This provides an account of Anthony rallying in favor of big bands after the decline of disco-music popularity.
8. For further information regarding his family's Italian heritage see Henry Mancini with Gene Lees, *Did They Mention the Music?* (Chicago: Contemporary Books, 1989), 1–12.
9. Mancini, *Did They Mention the Music?*, 16.
10. See James Wierzbicki, *Film Music: A History* (New York: Routledge, 2009), p. 208.
11. Bloom and Feinstein, *American Songbook*, 174, 226, 227, 259, 270.
12. David Bakish, *Jimmy Durante: His Show Business Career, with an Annotated Filmography and Discography* (Jefferson, North Carolina: McFarland, 2007).
13. Rotella, *Amore*, 148–149.
14. *New York Times*, November 26, 2003.
15. Mark Rotella, "Straight Out of Newark," *New York Times,* October 2, 2005; Rotella *Amore,* 238–240.
16. Rich Dyer *Nino Rota*: Music, *Film and Feeling* (New York : Palgrave Macmillan on behalf of theBritish Film Institute, 2010); and Mervyn

Cooke, *A History of Film Music* (New York, Cambridge University Press, 2008).

17. For more regarding the association of Morriconi and spaghetti films see Cooke, *A History of Film Music*, 371–372.

18. Cooke, *A History of Film Music*, 491. Beltrami's proficiency and versatility made him one of the most highly-regard composers.

CHAPTER 5

DIRECTORS, PRODUCERS, AND SCREENPLAY WRITERS

Many factors go into the successful making of a film: story line, script, actors, costumes, music, lighting, directors and producers, among others. It has been observed that the relationship between a producer and director is akin to a baseball owner and manager: the producer is concerned with the selection of a screenplay; financing; hiring key personnel, including the director; and the overall completion of the project. The director, on the other hand, establishes the inner meaning of the script and directs the film according to his or her own idea of how the story should play itself out; the end product reflects the director's vision of the unfolding of the plot. The director has a say in the actors to be employed in the film, how they should speak their lines, the emotions that are desirable, their physical position in scenes, the film locations in which to shoot the scenes, the way camera technicians should film their subjects, and the like. The most gifted directors are creative, sometimes modifying the original script, while at other times they must insist that actors conform to their ideas.

Among the few movie directors of Italian ancestry in the early years of moviemaking was Robert G. Vignola, born in the Basilicata region of

Italy in 1882 and raised in upstate New York. One description stated that he came from "humble Italian parentage, had a brain in his head, and was ambitious." He became an actor in 1906 and was most notable for his role of Judas Iscariot in *From the Manger to the Cross* (1912).[1] Subsequently, he became screenwriter and director, primarily during the silent screen era, during which he directed many of the films of Pauline Frederick, a popular actress of her day who starred in his production of *Audrey* (1916). With the advent of talkies, he directed a few films, including *Broken Dreams* (1933) and *The Girl From Scotland Yard* (1937). Vignola died in 1953 and was buried in St. Agnes Cemetery in Menands, New York.

Frank Borzage, of Swiss, Italian, and Austrian ancestry, was born in 1893 in Salt Lake City, Utah, one of eight children of an Italian-speaking stonemason father and a German-speaking mother. The religious influences on his life were problematic in that, although the family was Roman Catholic, he was never baptized. Furthermore, he grew up in heavily Mormon surroundings. He entered the movie industry first as an actor in silent films, and then as a director. His first movie in that capacity, *Humoresque* (1920), was a film about Jewish life in New York City. In the 1920s he produced and directed several films, winning major acclaim with *Seventh Heaven* (1927) and earning an Academy Award for Best Director for his ability to draw naturalness out of his actors. This film brought fame to Janet Gaynor and Charles Farrell for their portrayal of romantic lovers, as did their subsequent roles in *Street Angel* (1928) and *Lucky Star* (1929), also directed by Borzage. He won his second Academy Award for Best Director for *Bad Girl* (1931). Although Borzage continued to direct movies through the 1950s, critics considered that he had approached the quality of his earlier works only in *Moonrise* (1948). He was married once to actress Lorena Rogers and died of cancer, in 1962 at age sixty-eight.[2]

Born in Bisacquino, Sicily, in 1897 as Frank Rosario Capra, he immigrated to the United States as a child with his parents, Turiddu and Rosaria Capra, and three siblings to join an older brother in California—the family would grow to seven children. He attended California public schools, and after his father died Frank worked at odd jobs in order to go to college, where he received a chemical engineering degree. He joined the Army during the First World War, achieving the rank of lieutenant, and became a naturalized American citizen. Upon discharge, he began working behind the scenes in the fledgling movie industry, where he learned about props, editing, and film direction; a useful background to his subsequent writing and directing of silent film comedies, which won him acclaim. Capra soon became the top director for the Columbia Pictures organization. He won his first Academy Award as Best Director for his 1934 screwball comedy, *It Happened One Night*, which he also coproduced with Harry Cohn and whose script was previously rejected by several Hollywood actors but nonetheless became an Academy Award–winning vehicle for the stars Claudette Colbert and Clark Gable. Capra won his second Best Director Academy Award for *Mr. Deeds Goes to Town* (1936) and his third such award for *You Can't Take it With You* (1938).

Altogether, Frank Capra won six Academy Awards, three for Best Director within five years, two for Outstanding Production and one for Best Documentary—the latter award was for his work during the Second World War in which he served as a major in the Army Signal Corps. During this period he produced the award-winning, seven-part series *Why We Fight*, a highly effective propaganda documentary collection, which he regarded as his best work and for which he was honored with the Distinguished Service Medal. Among Capra's other memorable films that have stood the test of the ages were *Arsenic and Old Lace* (1944), *Mr. Smith Goes to Washington* (1939), and the perennial Christmas favorite *It's a Wonderful Life* (1946). The latter movie was produced by Liberty Films, a company started by directors Capra, William Wyler and George Stevens as an independent filmmaking company that would not have to deal with annoying interference from the movie moguls who owned other studios. Ironically, *It's a Wonderful Life,* the only movie the firm produced, did not initially seem to be a success but subsequently became a quintessential "feel good" winner. In the 1950s, Capra also made several documentaries on science which expressed concern over global warming and which have been used for classroom instruction. Capra was also credited with writing the screenplay for the film *Westward the Women* (1951), which depicts the trials, tribulations and triumphs of 140 nineteenth-century women pioneers who travel to the American west to marry lonely miners. Apparently too busy to direct it himself, Capra turned to his associate William Wellman to serve as the film's director. Capra is considered one of the very top directors of all time for his innovations and skill in movie making, his populist portrayals, the simplicity of his story lines, and especially his masterful depiction of the simple man who tries to fight corruption in society. Although he did not escape criticism for over-sentimentality, he is nevertheless credited with reflecting the worth of the individual in a way that resonated with audiences because what he offered on the screen promoted a sense of responsibility. Because the success of his films revolves around main characters faced with moral crises— the classic confrontation between the idealist and the villain—critics of Capra's films have debated the issue of whether his religious background influenced the moral vision in his movies. The prevailing consensus is that the power and consistency of the filmmaker's moral vision are, in effect, reflections of his own experiences. Although he initially did not practice the Catholicism of his birth, the combination of his inner conversion and the influence of his wife Lucille Reyburn, gradually led to a return to the Catholic fold. Thus he described the religion of his younger days as that of being a Christmas Catholic, that is, a nominal Catholic, but one who was nevertheless continually attracted to the magnetism of Catholicism, as when on holy days, "I would sneak into a Catholic church to kneel, to smell the incense, hear the angels sing, and be lifted out of my shoes by the passion and resurrection of Christ."[3]

In 1923 Capra married actress Helen Edith Howe. However, the marriage did not last. His second wife, Lucille Warner Reyburn, was the mother of his four children, one of whom, Frank Capra Jr., worked as a movie producer, while his grandson Frank Capra III became a director. In 1991, Frank Capra died at age ninety-four.[4]

Vincente Minnelli was an extraordinarily talented Italian American director whose career bridged the era between Hollywood's "Golden Age" and the end of the extravaganza type of productions. Born in 1903 in Chicago as Lester Anthony Minnelli to a mother of French-Canadian descent and a father of Sicilian heritage, he later changed his name to Vincente in honor of his father, who earned a living as the conductor of a touring musical group. Early in life, young Vincente worked as a photographer of actors and a designer of sets and costumes in Chicago theaters. He moved to New York, where he became a director of stage musical reviews that featured famous show-business stars, until he was hired by MGM Motion Pictures to direct films, beginning with *Cabin in the Sky* (1943) and *Meet Me in St Louis* (1944); the latter starred Judy Garland, to whom he was married for a short period, during which he became the father of actress Liza Minnelli.

Backed by the resources of a major studio, Vincente went on to make a number of lavish and memorable, mid-century, musical extravaganzas including *An American in Paris* (1951), for which he received an Oscar nomination for Best Director; *Brigadoon* (1954); *Kismet* (1955); and his film *Gigi* (1958) for which he won the Oscar for Best Director.[5]

In his direction of film, Minnelli saw his role as a type of magician, an enchanter leading the viewers to a world of romance, fairy tale and myth. Drawing upon European high-class and bohemian trends, Minnelli is credited with introducing modernist developments within the arts to Hollywood movies and synthesizing them into a distinctly American product.[6] His success with musicals tended to overshadow his genuine ability to direct romantic comedies like *The Courtship of Eddie's Father* (1953), as well as strong dramatic films that resulted in Academy Awards for many stars in films such as *The Bad and the Beautiful* (1952).

The Italian ancestry of Francis Ford Coppola derives from both his mother's side and that of his father, whose parents emigrated from the Basilicata region. The second of three children, Francis was born in 1939 in Detroit, where his father played in a symphony orchestra. When the family moved to Queens, New York City, he went to P.S. 109 elementary school—an education interrupted by a severe and traumatizing attack of polio during which he could not interact with other children and learned to entertain himself by watching television and learning to use a movie projector and a tape recorder.[7] As a youngster, he showed strong interest in film and when the family moved to New York, he enrolled in Hofstra University's theater program and then studied film direction while earning a Master's Degree in Fine Arts at the Los Angeles campus of The University of California. Initially producing short films, he made a major impact when he wrote the screenplay for the blockbuster award-winning movie Patton (1970) which earned him an Academy Award for Best Original Screenplay.[8] Coppola so highly valued his Hofstra experience that he founded the Hofstra Cinema Workshop.

Coppola made history in 1972 when he served as director of and, in collaboration with author Mario Puzo, wrote the screenplay for, The Godfather, one of the biggest money-making movies of all time. The film won three Academy Awards, one for Best Picture, another for Best Actor (Marlon Brando) and one for Best Adapted Screenplay awarded to Coppola. One of the unique aspects of Coppola's film was the extensive use of family members: his two sons and a daughter, for example, appear as extras in The Godfather while his sister Talia Shire had a major role as Connie Corleone, and Carmine Coppola, his musician father, is credited with composing much of the film's music. It has been pointed out that even though the production was made on a low budget, Coppola's brilliance rendered it a work of art. "Coppola created a classic dramatic narrative that resembles the traditional five-stages of a classical play."[9] The critically acclaimed Godfather Part II (1974) proved to be an equally successful movie, winning six Academy Awards including Best Picture, making it the first sequel to win the Academy Award for Best Picture; Best Supporting Actor for Robert De Niro; Best Adapted Screenplay; and Best Director for Coppola. Godfather Part III (1990), the third in the Godfather trilogy directed by Coppola, was financially successful and was nominated for several Oscars but failed to win any significant awards. One analysis of the last film in the Godfather series likens it to grand opera in that while Michael Corleone searches for legitimacy and redemption, what awaits him is more tragedy.[10]

Coppola was also successful as a Hollywood movie producer, a fact evidenced by his film *American Grafitti* (1973), a coming-of-age film costing less than a million dollars which depicted the lives of young people in the California of the 1960s and which was nominated for the Academy Award for Best Picture along with nominations for Best Director, Best Original Screenplay, Best Supporting Actress and Best Film Editing. Although it did not win in these categories, it influenced the making of other films of that era that focused on young people and with subsequent releases was reported to have earned a staggering 118 million dollars. Francis, however, continued to direct Hollywood films ,including *The Conversation* (1974), for which he also wrote the script, which received nomination for a Best Picture Academy Award, thereby rendering Coppola one of the few directors to have two films competing with each other for that award in the same year, the other being *Godfather Part II*. Other films directed by Coppola include *Apocalypse Now* (1979), a sturdy, culturally significant film about the Vietnam War that won critical praise but proved to be so costly it nearly bankrupted the studio, *The Cotton Club* (1984), *Peggy Sue Got Married* (1986), which starred his nephew Nicholas Cage, and *Dracula* (1992). In 1969 Coppola and George Lucas founded American Zoetrope, a film studio that was an early adopter of digital filmmaking. The studio has produced many of the films of both men as well as those of Coppola's daughter Sofia. A highly successful business that is now owned by Francis' children, it is headquartered in an older Italian section of San Francisco and has produced films that have received fifteen Academy Awards and sixty-eight nominations. In addition to movies, Coppola has also delved into different businesses, at times coowning restaurants and establishing a winery.

In recent years, he has sought to reconnect with his Italian heritage by doing something about the small town from which his forbears came.

"Ever since I first visited, during the early 1960s, I have always wanted to do something for my family's hometown," he said. This may well have been the background to his participation in the 2007 Roman Film Festival, where the first film he directed after a hiatus of ten years, *Youth Without Youth*, was premiered but met with mixed reviews.[11] Now in his seventies, Coppola continues to write and direct movies such as *Tetro* (2009), a tale of two brothers reuniting with a talented but irascible father. The movie, filmed in Argentina, encountered delays and obstacles before it was finally released. Although some critics cited flaws in the production it received generally positive reviews. A forthcoming film which he produced, wrote and directed is a gothic horror film, called *Twixt,* scheduled to be released in 2011. Coppola is married to Eleanor, who is also accomplished at screenwriting and directing, and is the mother of his three children, two of whom survive: Roman Coppola, a filmmaker and music video director, and daughter Sofia Coppola, an Academy Award–winning writer and Academy Award-nominated director.

Arguably, Martin Scorsese is considered to be the most significant and influential film director of our time. He was born in New York City in 1942 to Italian American parents who worked in the garment industry; his father Luciano was a pants presser, while his mother Catherine was a seamstress. As a youngster, he was enamored of movies, especially influenced by Italian neo-realistic films of the 1950s.[12] Because of his family's ethnic roots, he was said to be partial to movies depicting Sicilian life and culture. While in Cardinal Hayes High School in the Bronx, he gave thought to becoming a priest but abandoned the idea as he became more involved in cinema activity after attending New York University, where he received his Master's in Fine Arts, specializing in film directing. He began making short films and also made the acquaintance of highly regarded film makers like John Cassavetes, and other aspirants in the field. His direction of the movie *Mean Streets* (1973) proved to be particularly meaningful for Martin and the actors who were cast in the key parts: Robert De Niro and Harvey Keitel. The religious nexus of *Mean Streets* has been cited as being so palpable as to be able to describe it virtually as a religious film.

A writer explains "it was the Roman Catholic Church that shaped young Martin Scorsese," and even the director himself confessed the movie was a "religious statement."[13] Critics liked *Mean Streets* for its gritty, glamorless, and unadorned portrayal of New York urban life circa 1970. It demonstrated Scorsese's ability to elicit macho attitudes from his actors intermixed with violence, Catholic guilt and redemption. The movie was simultaneously praised for his skillful editing and soundtrack, specifically the use of contemporary music rather than music deliberately made for gangster movies as was the usual practice. "In our neighborhood you'd hear rock'n' roll playing in the little bars in the back of the tenement buildings at three in the morning."[14] *Mean Streets* has that ring of authenticity because in fact it was based on actual events Scorsese saw almost regularly while growing up in Little Italy and prompted a writer to comment "Some characters are permitted to flee this ethnic island that seems frozen in time; others are destined to remain there."[15]

Scorsese's *Taxi Driver* (1976) won critical acclaim for its depiction of a man's psychological deterioration as well as for the innovative cinematographic style employed. Robert De Niro plays the role of a mentally unstable Vietnam War veteran who drives a taxi at night and upon witnessing the degradation that takes place in the world of teenage prostitution, becomes obsessed with his mission to eliminate the causes of sleaze and squalor. It was nominated for four Oscars and was also cited as having influenced John Hinckley Jr., who attempted to assassinate President Ronald Reagan.

The scope of films directed by Scorsese is vast, encompassing movies ranging from the depiction the genteel nineteenth century high society in *The Age of Innocence* (1993) to films of extreme violence such as *Goodfellas* (1995) and *Casino* (1995). He also has engaged in a search for his ethnic roots as illustrated in *Italianamerican* (1974) a documentary that revolves around his parents' lives as prototypical, Roman Catholic immigrants in post–World War II New York City. While some have hailed it for its penetrating portrayal of Italian American life in the tenements, others regard it as little better than a homemade movie that has been praised because it was made by a famous and successful movie maker.

Scorsese has directed numerous films that have received Oscar nominations in which actors earned Academy Awards. These include Ellen Burstyn in *Alice Doesn't Live Here Anymore* (1974), Robert De Niro in *Raging Bull* (1980), Paul Newman in *The Color of Money* (1986), Joe Pesci in *Goodfellas* (1990), and Cate Blanchett in *The Aviator* (2004). In addition, his films have resulted in Academy Awards for others in the fields of Costume Design, Art Direction, Cinematography, Best Original Song, Screenplay and Film Editing. Although he was nominated for the Best Director Academy Award several times it was not until 2006 that he won the celebrated award for his movie *The Departed*, a crime film with a formidable cast which won four Oscars (Best Picture, Best Director, Best Film Editing, and Best Adopted Screenplay) as well as a nomination for Best Supporting Actor. Furthermore, several of his films have been included in a listing of the greatest films of all time. Scorsese continues to be a productive and award-winning filmmaker, as reflected in his 2010 production of *Shutter Island* and the HBO series *Boardwalk Empire* (2010).[16]

Long Island, New York was the birthplace of Albert R. Broccoli in 1909; his Italian American family then moved to Florida. He boasted, in an unsubstantiated claim, that in the 1870s his uncle introduced Americans to the vegetable that bears his name. As a young man he had an assortment of menial jobs until he became involved in the movie industry allowing him to meet many celebrities such as Wallace Beery, Howard Hughes and Henry Salzman. He also became embroiled in some of the seamier episodes of Hollywood, including teaming up with his notorious cousin Pat DiCicco and the actor Wallace Beery in a barroom brawl that left a man dead.

After a stint in the Navy during World War II, Broccoli worked for several years as an agent, a production crew member, assistant director, director and producer doing several films a year and linking up with other ambitious film makers. One of these contacts resulted in his moving to London where, together with Irving Allen, he formed the Warwick Films Company, which brought together a partnership of Henry Salzman and Albert Broccoli which, in 1962, began to produce James Bond films. After the partnership dissolved, Broccoli continued to produce the highly popular James Bond movies that meant stardom for the likes of Sean Connery and Roger Moore. Broccoli's mother shared in her son's success, especially thrilled to see the Broccoli name on local movie marquees.[17] In recognition of the success of his film work the 1981 Academy Award ceremony extended the Irving G. Thalberg Memorial Award to Broccoli. Albert was married three times and had three children. He died in Beverly Hills, California at age eighty-seven in 1996.

Producer, director and cartoon artist Joseph Roland Barbera, born to Sicilian immigrants Vincent Barbera and Frances Calvacca in 1911 in New York's Little Italy, became one of the greatest film animators in Hollywood history. Growing up, he spoke Italian and together with his family moved to Brooklyn, where his father operated several successful barber shops but who, sadly, squandered his money and abandoned the family. By the age of eight, Joseph exhibited such exceptional drawing ability that the nuns at Holy Innocents Catholic elementary school gave him the task of drawing Christ's entry into Jerusalem on the class black-board in colored chalks. Joseph's interest in drawing continued at Erasmus High School where he drew cartoons for the school newspaper while also becoming active in sports. Additionally, he demonstrated his talent at the Art Students League of New York and at the Pratt Institute before obtaining employment as an animator. He moved to California in 1937 to work in that capacity for MGM Studios, where he met Bill Hanna—a fortuitous meeting which would soon result in a partnership that would last sixty years and produce the immensely popular *Tom and Jerry* cartoon series. The series won its first Academy Award for *The Yankee Doodle Mouse* (1943), followed by *Mouse Trouble* (1944), *Quiet Please* (1945), *The Cat Concerto* (1946), *The Little Orphan* (1948), *Two Mouseketeers* (1951), and *Johann Mouse* (1952). The *Tom and Jerry* series was ultimately nominated for fourteen Academy Awards, winning seven, a feat unsurpassed by any other character-based theatrical animated series.[18] Their cartoon production was so ubiquitous that it became familiar not only to movie-goers but also to television audiences, who were amused by such cartoon characters as *Yogi Bear*, *Huckleberry Hound*, *The Flintstones* and *The Jetsons*. Barbera lived to the ripe old age of ninety-five; he died in 2006, leaving his wife Sheila and three children from a previous marriage.

Born in 1946 in New York City, Sylvester Gardenzio Stallone was the son of Frank Stallone, Sr., a hairdresser, and Jackie Stallone, an astrologer and former dancer.[19] Because of his parents' marital problems, Sylvester lived in various locations including Queens, New York, Silver Springs, Maryland, and foster homes. Seemingly not enthralled with school he did, however, enroll in the Theater Department at the University of Miami, tried his hand a screenwriting and had bit parts, usually uncredited, in unremarkable movies. Sylvester was not having much success until he wrote the script for the film *Rocky* (1976) in which he played the lead part as Rocky Balboa, a nobody from the streets who became a champion prizefighter. The movie proved to be an instant success, garnering ten Academy Award nominations and winning three, including the Academy Awards for Best Picture, Best Editing, and Best Directing. It became the highest-grossing film of the year and established Stallone as a major star. Shot in Philadelphia, the city has built a statue of his Rocky character and placed it on permanent display near a museum. *Rocky* was also inducted into the National Film Registry. The success of the original naturally suggested sequels, with Stallone serving as director, writer and star for *Rocky II* (1979), *Rocky III* (1982), and others in the genre.[20]

Stallone's directorial debut came with the production of *Paradise Alley* (1978), for which he served as writer, director, and star in this film about three Italian American brothers growing up in New York's Hell's Kitchen in the 1940s, whose goals were to become professional wrestlers. He likewise directed, wrote, and acted in *Rambo* (2008), a story of a group of mercenaries fighting to save Christian missionaries in war torn Burma, which was a sequel to other Rambo movies in which he acted. Stallone continues to write, direct, produce, and act, as evidenced by his 2010 production *The Expendables*, a tale of muscular mercenaries on a mission to oust a ruthless dictatorship in Latin America, featuring the likes of Arnold Schwarzenegger and Bruce Willis.

Stallone has been married three times and is the father of five children. After years of success and celebrity status he has undergone a self-evaluation and returned to religion. Accordingly, in recent years he has resumed his religious life and is once again a churchgoing Catholic.

Among the current generation of screenwriters, directors and producers of Italian ancestry, Quentin Jerome Tarantino stands out as one of the most talented. Born in 1963 in Knoxville, Tennessee, to a mother of Irish American and Cherokee Indian ancestry and a father of Italian descent, he was raised by his mother, who moved to California, where he went to local schools. As a young man he worked in a video rental store, watching movies continually and relishing the task of recommending films to customers, while additionally writing screenplays. In the 1980s he also became an independent filmmaker and had a major breakthrough with his 1992 film *Reservoir Dogs*, which he wrote and directed, and which won critical acclaim, thereby entering the cult film annals. Featuring a nonlinear story line, the movie about a robbery gone wrong is characterized by scenes of violence, blood, gore, and profanity. In answer to the question of whether the violence shown in his films abets societal violence, Tarantino responds that his violence is not harmful and that "as an artist, violence is part of my talent," and therefore he cannot start thinking about the possibility of encouraging it in society.[21] Tarantino cowrote and directed *Pulp Fiction* (1994), a critical and commercial success (earning over one hundred million dollars) that was nominated for seven Academy Awards; it earned Tarantino and his coauthor an Academy Award for Best Screenplay. Tarantino won the Academy Award for Best Director for *Inglourious Basterds* (2009) a movie about Jewish American soldiers spreading fear in Nazi Germany. In his mid-forties, Tarantino has been romantically linked with several women but remains unmarried.

In reviewing the role which Italian Americans have played and currently play as directors and producers, it becomes evident that, whereas in Hollywood's early years there were but a few in those influential positions, the situation has changed dramatically. In addition to the above-named individuals, one can cite many more who have made their mark in that regard. Born in New York City in 1939, Michael Cimino graduated from high school in Old Westbury, New York and went on to study at Yale University. After graduating with a Master of Fine Arts degree he moved to California to pursue work in motion pictures. He enjoyed huge success with *The Deer Hunter* (1978) a powerful story about the Vietnam War that won Cimino three Academy Awards for Best Director, Best Picture, and Best Screenplay. Notwithstanding the fact that the film dealt with young men of Eastern European heritage who served in the Vietnam War, one critic maintains that Cimino "continues the tradition of discussing indirectly the more negative aspects of the American experience for Italian Americans."[22] Although he directed other films, he also alienated Hollywood moguls because of the huge cost of production of the movie *Heaven's Gate* (1980), which came in several times over original cost estimates and nearly bankrupted a major studio.

Brian De Palma was born to Italian Catholic parents but apparently not raised as a Catholic. He has worked as a film director for many years and was acknowledged as a gifted visual stylist. While critics pan some of his works he has also won acclaim for others. For example, his direction of *The Untouchables* (1987), based on the popular television series, was a commercial success and won an Academy Award for Best Actor for Sean Connery.

Among directors of Italian ancestry, mention must be made of several women, foremost of whom is Ida Lupino. Born to an acting family in England, Ida came to Hollywood and began making a major impression with her acting in the movies of the 1940s. However, a protracted contract dispute and suspension led her to work as a writer and director, essentially the kind of work she preferred. For a time, she was a partner in Emerald Productions, which became known as The Filmmakers, and which produced eight movies, with Ida directing six of them. Her first effort at directing was on the film *Not Wanted* (1949), for which she wrote the screenplay. Because severe illness incapacitated the original director she also filled in as director. Among other films she directed were *Outrage* (1950), which dealt with rape and its aftermath, and *The Bigamist* (1953) concerning issues that arise over attempts at child adoption. Lupino's directorial talents were also brought to television screens when she directed many episodes of *Kraft Suspense Theater* and *Panic*.[23]

Penny Marshall whose mother was of English and Scottish descent and whose father of was of Italian ancestry (he changed his last name from Marsciarelli to Marshall before Penny's birth), was another actress who became a director. Born in the Bronx, New York in 1942, Penny graduated from Walton High School, attended the University of New Mexico and then moved to California to join her brother Garry Marshall, a producer.[24] She entered the world of television, achieving success with situation comedies like *Laverne and Shirley* and *Happy Days*. Her directorial efforts produced a number of films; including *Big* (1988), a fantasy about a boy who realizes his wish to be big and finds himself in an adult body; *Awakenings* (1990), a story about the lives of victims of an encephalitis epidemic, which was nominated for three Oscars; and *A League of Their Own* (1992), a comedy drama about the first female, professional, baseball league.

Of Sicilian ancestry, Barbara De Fina was born in 1949 in Weehawken, New Jersey and attended but left Barnard College of Columbia University to work in the field that was an enduring magnet for her—theater. Her behind-the-scenes work included overseeing costuming, serving as a production assistant making commercials, and finally acting as executive producer of some important films in recent years. Content to work out of the spotlight, her activities involve lining up actors and film locations, reviewing scripts with writers, and working out contracts. She was married to Martin Scorsese for seven years and collaborated with him as executive producer of many films, such as the Oscar-winning *Goodfellas* (1990), along with *Cape Fear* (1991), *The Age of Innocence* (1993), *Casino* (1995), and *Kundin* (1997).

The daughter of Academy Award–winning director Francis Ford Coppola, Sofia Carmina Coppola, who was born New York City in 1971, is another example of an actress who became a director. Appearing in a number of films produced by her father, she began to write screenplays by the late 1990s, and to direct and produce films in her own name. Sofia received considerable attention with her first two films: *Lick the Star* (1998), a short film about four girls intent on poisoning boys in their school, and *The Virgin Suicides* (1999), a story about young men obsessed with three sisters. However, she really made film history with *Lost in Translation* (2003), for which she both wrote the screenplay and directed and which involves a male movie star and a married woman who meet in a Tokyo hotel. She won an Academy Award for Best Original Screenplay, and was nominated for Best Director, becoming only the third female to be so honored. Sofia developed her craft so well that her father Francis learned certain techniques from her, namely how to shoot on a more intimate scale while telling stories of family honor.[25]

Mark Alan Ruffalo, one of four children, born in Kenosha, Wisconsin in 1967, is the son of Marie Rose, a hair dresser of French Canadian heritage and Frank Lawrence Ruffalo Jr., a construction painter of Italian descent. Until his teenage years, when the family began having financial difficulties, Mark enjoyed a happy childhood amidst the joys of a large Italian family and attended the local Catholic Church and Catholic school as well as a progressive school. Because of the need to find work, the family moved frequently, including to California, where Mark attended the Stella Adler Conservatory and where he cofounded the Orpheus Theater Company, occupying his time writing, directing and starring in a number of plays while supplementing his income as a bartender. His entry into film acting began with minor roles in movies like *The Dentist*

(1966) and *Safe Men* (1998), however, it was his impressive and praise-worthy appearance in the play *This is Our Youth* (1998) which rewarded him with a major part in the Academy Award–winning film *You Can Count on Me* (2000). He also had roles in *Collateral* (2004), *Just Like Heaven* (2005), and *Rumor Has It* (2005). In 2011 he received a Best Supporting Actor Academy Award nomination for his role in *The Kids are All Right* (2010). Ruffalo has also worked at screenwriting with his production of *The Destiny of Marty Fine* (1996).

Mark Ruffalo made his directorial debut in the film *Sympathy for Delicious* (2010) that recounts the life of Dean, a recent paraplegic who one day wakes up to find he has the power of healing, except that he cannot heal himself. Ruffalo, playing the part of a kind priest, befriends Dean and encourages him to use his God-given gift to help others. The fact that the gritty storyline of *Sympathy for Delicious* was written by Christopher Thornton, a recent paraplegic and personal friend of Ruffalo renders it even more poignant. The movie had its premiere at the Sundance Film Festival, the pre-eminent showcase for independent films, where it won the Special Jury Prize in 2010. Ruffalo savors the director role because it puts him into contact with the entire film enterprise, not just a slice of it, as when he is working solely as an actor. He also acquires satisfaction that comes from the ability of a director to use the script to help actors realize their full potential. In addition to moviemaking, Mark Ruffalo has come to public attention for controversial views on public issues like the Iraq War, which he opposed, and gas drilling. He has had his share of personal stress, including overcoming a very serious brain tumor and the sudden death of a brother. He is married to French actress Sunrise Coigney and has three children.[26]

Among the contemporary Italian Americans who are active and successful as film producers are Dana Brunetti and Michael De Luca, who were part of the producing team for *The Social Network*, a film which was nominated for Best Picture of the Year in 2011. Born in 1973, Dana is the son of a retired mail carrier who moved from New Jersey to

Kentucky, where Dana was raised in the town of Covington and where he went to school. Upon graduation, he joined the U. S. Coast Guard and upon completing his tenure, went into the cell phone business. A chance meeting with actor Kevin Spacey and attendance at New York University's Film School led to Dana's growing involvement in the moviemaking industry, eventually becoming president of Trigger Street Productions. He has produced several films, including *Beyond The Sea* (2004), *Fanboys* (2009), and *The Social Network* (2010). [27]

Born in Brooklyn in 1965, Michael De Luca is the son of a working-class, Italian Catholic father and a Jewish, Holocaust survivor mother. Attracted neither to athletic nor intellectual pursuits, he became deeply interested in films, attended New York University's Film School, and began a career as a screenwriter and producer commencing as an associate producer of *Leatherface: The Texas Chainsaw Massacre III* (1988). He served as president in charge of production for New Line Cinema, president of Dreamworks, and then headed his own company, Michael De Luca Productions, which produced *Ghost Rider* (2007) and *The Love Guru* (2008), prior to his involvement with *The Social Network*.[28]

Born in 1968, in West Islip, Long Island, New York, Ken Marino (Kenneth Joseph Marino), the son, grandson and nephew of clam diggers, graduated from New York University's Tisch School of the Arts with a Bachelor of Fine Arts specializing in drama and has been at various times an actor, comedian, director, producer, screenwriter, and composer. After honing his craft in school productions and off-Broadway shows, he was instrumental in founding the group that wrote *The State,* which gained a following on MTV. He soon followed this with feature roles in such television series as *Men Behaving Badly* and *First Years* and a recurring role on *Dawson's Creek*, and then began to appear in films like *Gattaca* (1997), *Wet Hot American Summer* (2001), and *Tortilla Soup* (2001).

With his movie *Diggers* (2007), Marino demonstrated theatrical abilities that extended beyond acting into the realm of writing scripts and producing movies. A coming-of-age film that reflects the difficulty of

earning a livelihood experienced by his own family, which was victim-
ized by a big business that bought up rights to the most productive clam
areas, *Diggers* is the story of Long island clam diggers striving against the
odds as they troll the bottom waters off the South Shore of Long Island
in search of a depleted and shrinking shellfish source. Marino is one the
principal actors in the movie that led one reviewer to comment about the
film's integrity;

> If the four friends and the women in their lives make up a stereo-
> typical cross-section of thirtysomethings, the seamless ensemble
> acting and the way the screenplay captures the deeper realities
> bared in offhanded conversation make the characters seem alive
> and spontaneous.[29]

Subsequently, Marino has cowritten, coproduced and appeared in the
following movies: *The Ten* (2007) and *Role Models* (2008). He is married
and has one child.

   Italian Americans in the cinema industry may seem to have been more
prominent as actors and directors and sometimes producers, however,
a number of them interacted with Hollywood as script writers, though
admittedly much later than other ethnic groups, like Jewish Americans.
"Italian Americans did not hold leading roles in the industry...not until the
1930s did Italian American writers begin publishing in English."[30] The
first major example was writer John Fante, the son of a seeming mismatch
of parents: Nick, a hard-drinking Italian immigrant father from Abbruzzi
and Mary, a Chicago-born, timid, deeply religious mother. John was Show
lessborn in 1909 in Denver, Colorado, and raised in Boulder, where he
went to Catholic elementary and secondary schools and briefly attended
the University of Colorado. John brought with him a heritage of poverty
and prejudice when he left Colorado at age twenty for Los Angeles, determined to become a great writer. A prolific author, his talent was rewarded
by publication of short stories in eminent national magazines, though he
preferred to focus on novels, often meeting dispiriting rejection before a
publishing house produced what is considered his most significant work,

Ask The Dust. It is a semi-autobiographical account of Arturo Bandini, essentially his alter ego, which became a part of a series of books about Bandini, such as *The Road to Los Angeles*, *Wait Until Spring Bandini*, and *Full of Life*. He married Joyce Smart, a Stanford University poet and editor who was strongly supportive and who bore his four children. In time he came to be regarded as "one of Los Angeles's most original and engaging writers."[31]

Unfortunately, writing novels brought an insufficient income and thus he turned to writing screenplays to earn a living. Despite the fact that he met and worked with the likes of Orson Welles, he deemed it hack work. Nevertheless, the leitmotifs of his literary production: Italian identity, Catholicism, poverty, and sports could be discerned in some of his screenplays, especially when he returned to working-class themes and the ethnic individual's struggle for upward mobility. Religion is one example. Unhesitatingly professing his Catholicism, it was not surprising to learn that he cowrote the script for the movie *The Reluctant Saint* (1962), a story based on the life of Italian St. Joseph Cupertino which, remarkably, was produced and directed by former blacklisted Communist Edward Dmytryk.

Among Fante's screenplays were *The Golden Fleecing* (1940); *East of the River* (1940); *Youth Runs Wild* (1944); *Full of Life* (1956), for which he wrote both the story and screenplay; *Jeanne Eagels* (1957); *Walk on the Wild Side* (1962); and *Maya* (1966). His screenplay for *Full of Life* was nominated for Best Written American Comedy at the 1957 Writers Guild of America conference. Ironically, although not fully appreciated in his time all of John Fante's works have been republished (or, in some instances, published for the first time) posthumously and he has come to be regarded as one of America's greatest writers. After his death in 1983 from the debilitating disease of diabetes, two of his books were made into films: *Wait Until Spring Bandini* (1989) and *Ask the Dust* (2006).[32]

John Hermes Secondari, born in Rome in 1919, came to the United States where he received his bachelor's degree from Fordham University in 1939, followed by a masters in journalism from Columbia University. After his Army service, in which he saw action during the Second World War, he returned to civilian life, became a writer and played a dominant role during television's early days working for the news department at ABC and becoming the executive in charge of the network's first regular documentary series. He and his wife created a film company which, in succeeding years, produced dozens of documentaries on historical topics. Although he had a lesser impact in Hollywood, he did write the script for the very popular film *Three Coins in the Fountain* (1954), which title also graced a famous song. The movie is about three American girls in Rome looking for romance. It won Academy Awards for Best Cinematography, Best Color and Best Music (for a song of the same title) and was nominated for Best Picture. He remarried after the death of his first wife, with whom he had a son, and died of a heart attack at age fifty-five in 1975.[33]

Theater, acting and entertainment were such strong magnets for Joseph Stefano that he left Philadelphia, where he was born in 1922 to Italian immigrants. Before he even finished high school, he departed for New York City, where he changed his name to Jerry Stevens, and wrote his own material, which he sang, danced and played on the piano in Greenwich Village clubs. He then began to write radio scripts and by the 1950s he had entered the cinema world, writing screenplays, first as a cowriter on *Anna of Brooklyn* (a.k.a. *Fast and Sexy*, 1958), an Italian, Vittorio De Sica production featuring Gina Lollobrigida. His solo screenplay writing was for the movie *The Black Orchid* (1959), in which he incorporated some ideas gleaned from his immigrant father, a tailor who made silk flowers. Stefano's biggest success came as a screenwriter for the revolutionary, blockbuster, thriller *Psycho* (1960), which came when famed director Alfred Hitchcock, unhappy with an earlier script, entrusted Stefano with the writing task that resulted in producing the classic film. Stefano's work on the film, which involved extensive rewriting, brought him an award from The Mystery Writers of America, as well as high compliments for writing the screenplay, based on a novel by Robert Bloch. When the script was reshot in the 1990s, one critic observed that it "remains a model of concision in its plotting and a repository of sinister vibrations in its dialogues. And, since the script hasn't been altered, here is a 1990s adult film without the F word."[34]

A much sought-after writer, Stefano also worked as a writer and producer of *The Outer Limits,* a highly regarded science-fiction television series. Mention must be made of the script Stefano wrote for *Two Bits* (1995), which he also produced and which was a partially autobiographical coming-of-age account of a young Italian American boy who is willing to do anything to get two bits (a quarter) from his ailing grandfather so he can go to the movies during a hot South Philadelphia summer day in 1933. Stefano continued to work as a screenplay writer for television shows and several movies, including a 1998 remake of *Psycho* under director, Gus Van Sant and died in 2006 at age eighty-four.[35]

Nicholas Pileggi, born in New York City in 1933 and raised in Bensonhurst, Brooklyn, is currently one of Hollywood's more successful screenwriters. The son of Susan and Nick (a shoe store owner) Pileggi, he began his writing career working part-time for the Associated Press, where he covered the crime beat while he attended Long Island University. He then became a contributing editor for *New York Magazine*, where he continued writing about crime and the Italian American community. This was the background to his nonfiction book *Wiseguys*, which told the story of low-level hoodlums in crime families in Italian American neighborhoods—a work that attracted the attention of director Martin Scorsese and that was transformed into the movie *Goodfellas* (1990) for which Pileggi served as coscreenwriter with Scorsese. The film proved highly successful at the box office and was nominated for six Academy Awards including Best Screenplay. Pileggi then wrote *Casino*, another nonfiction crime book that was a searing depiction of the glitter and glamour of Las Vegas as well as its brutal and cruel face. It became the basis for a stylish movie by the same name, for which Pileggi once again teamed up with Scorsese and wrote the screenplay—the venture led to an Academy Award nomination for Best Film. Pileggi was a writer for another Hollywood film, *City Hall*, (1996) a story loosely based on the turbulence of political life of New York City of the 1980s which featured a popular mayor, a near municipal bankruptcy, and ongoing corruption and scandal. Continuing to work in the cinematic crime genre, Pileggi was a coproducer of *The American Gangster* (2007). In 1987, Pileggi became the third husband of author Nora Ephron.[36]

Bronx-born Nancy Savoca (born in 1959) is the daughter of an Argentine mother and a Sicilian father who has become an active participant in the movie industry as an independent producer, director and screenplay writer. Having studied at Queens College, she graduated from New York University's Tisch School of Arts and made a strong impression with her 1989 debut movie *True Love*, a story about Italian American marriage rituals based on the lives of her parents. Savoca elicited even more positive reviews for her work in producing *Household Saints* (1993) for which she also rewrote the script together with her husband Richard Guay. *Household Saints*, which deals with religion and spirituality in the lives of three Italian American New Yorkers, received a nomination for Spirit Award for Best Screenplay for Savoca and Guay. Savoca continues to write television movies such as *If These Walls Could Talk* (1996), for which she also served as director. Nancy Savoca is married and the mother of three children.[37]

Jon Favreau (Jonathan Kolia Favreau) has combined careers as an actor, screenwriter and director. Born in 1966 in Flushing, Queens, to a Jewish mother and an father of French Canadian, Italian, and Catholic background, he appeared in films including the inspiring sports story *Rudy* (1993) and the comedy/drama *Swingers* (1996), written by him and for which he served as coproducer. His success prompted a critic to say, "Favreau is a genius when it comes to unexpected casting coups."[38] The recipient of critical acclaim for his direction of the Marvel comic book superhero film *Iron Man* (2008), Favreau has followed that up by becoming director of a big-budget thriller, *Cowboys and Aliens* (2011), thereby placing him alongside current leading directors of action films.

In the spring of 2011, The National Italian American Foundation honored him with a Special Achievement Award in Entertainment.

Screenwriter and film producer Angelo Pizzo is the son of a Sicilian immigrant and a native of Bloomington, Indiana where he went to school and earned a degree from Indiana University. He then attended the University of Southern California's film school, lived and worked in California and moved back to Bloomington. An avid basketball fan, when he was in his thirties he began his success as a screenwriter and in the process wrote the storyline for two of the most acclaimed sports films: *Hoosiers* (1987), about the centrality of basketball to the social life in a small town in Indiana, which received two Oscar nominations; and *Rudy* (1993) an account of the life of Daniel "Rudy" Ruettiger, who harbored dreams of playing football for Notre Dame. It was named one of the best sports movies in its era. For these movies, Pizzo created characters faced with obstacles who found ways to overcome them.[39] In 2009, Pizzo and director David Anspaugh attempted to obtain the same results in *Game of Their Lives* (2005), the story of an Italian American underdog soccer team from St. Louis entering the World Cup games and beating the favorite English team.

James DeMonaco is another example of a young Italian American making his mark in the cinema world as a behind-the-scenes contributor: writer, director, and producer. Born in Brooklyn, New York in 1969, James studied English and film as an undergraduate at Rutgers University, and was in the graduate program at New York University's film school when he wrote and produced a short film that won high student honors. Throughout his professional career, he has written both feature and television films, in which major actors have starred. He has written, among other movie scripts, the comedy/drama *Jack* (1996), directed by Francis Ford Coppola; the action film/thriller *Assault on Precinct 13* (2005)l and *Skinwalkers* (2006), a horror/action film about werewolves. DeMonaco also wrote and directed *Staten Island* (a.k.a. *Little New York*, 2009) a nonlinear, quirky, offbeat, crime film that met with mixed reviews, convincing the producers to offer it primarily as a DVD product.[40]

The importance of Italian Americans as directors, producers and screen-writers and conversely, their earlier paucity in the same categories, cannot be overestimated. One study asserts that their relative absence, until recently, from these prominent positions constituted "the single most important impediment to the removal of reductive stereotypes of Italians in movies ..."[41] Over the course of three generations of Hollywood film-making one can see a remarkable transformation when it comes to the role of those of Italian ancestry in the fields of directing, producing and screenwriting. Whereas in the early period of the film industry Italian Americans accounted for only a handful of participants in these fields, by the last third of the twentieth century and into the twenty-first century there were multiple examples. In addition to the above-named, they would include John Turturro, Raymond De Felitta, Garry Marshall, Danny De Vito, Vincent Gallo, Stanley Tucci, Isabella Rossellini, Nicholas Cage, David Chase, Vincent D'Onofrio, Maria Ripoli, Richard Vetere, Tina Scorzafava, Joseph Petrarca and Abel Ferrara, among others.

ENDNOTES

1. Linda A. Griffith, *When the Movies Were Young* (New York: Arno Press, 1977), 35.
2. Herve Dumont, *Frank Borzage: The Life and Films of a Hollywood Romantic* (Jefferson, North Carolina: McFarland, 2009).
3. Capra, *The Name Above the Title*, 130.
4. George Stevens, Jr., *Conversations With The Great Movie Makers of Hollywood's Golden Age* (New York: Alfred A. Knopf, 2006), 77.
5. Hollywood producers of musicals showed a marked favoritism for Minnelli's direction and his ability to extract the essence of characterization from actors. See Hugh Fordin, *M-G-M's Greatest Musicals* (New York: De Capo Press, 1996), 206–207.
6. Joe McElhaney *The Death of Classical Cinema: Lang, Hitchcock, Minnelli* (Albany: SUNY University Press, 2006), 148.
7. Linda Brandi Cateura, *Growing Up Italian* (New York: William Morrow, 1987), 75–81. See also Gene D. Philips, *Godfather*, (Lexington, Kentucky: The University of Kentucky Press, 2004), 8–9.
8. Philip, *Godfather*, 10. Coppola so highly valued his Hofstra experience that he founded the Hofstra Cinema Workshop.
9. Bondanella, *Hollywood Italians*, 251.
10. Bondanella, *Hollywood Italians*, 266.
11. Nick Vivarelli, *Variety*, June 21, 2004; *Daily Variety*, October 22, 2007.
12. One example of this influence can be found in Maricia Sellari, "Dream and Life Companionship And Loneliness in Fellini and Scorsese," *The Italian American Review* 5, no. 2 (Autumn/Winter 1996/1997): 71–78.
13. Friedman, Lawrence S., *The Cinema of Martin Scorsese*, (New York: Continuum, 1997), 10. Even though it treats of Buddhistic spiritual matters, it has been asserted that Scorsese's movie *Kundun* "bears the imprint of his Italian American and his Italian Catholic origins." Robert Casillo, "Scorsese in the Land of Snows: The Splendor of Kundun," *Italian Americana* 17, no. 1 (Winter 1999): 14–35.
14. Bondanella, *Hollywood Italians*, 80–81
15. Bondanella, *Hollywood Italians*, 77; Richard Schikel, *Conversations With Scorsese* (New York: Knopf, 2011) makes much reference to growing up in a tough neighborhood.

16. Roger Ebert, *Scorsese by Ebert* (Chicago: The University of Chicago Press, 2009).

17. Broccoli, Albert, *When the Snow Melts: The Autobiography of Cubby Broccoli* (London: Boxtree, 1999), 137.

18. Jeff Lenburg, *The Encyclopedia of Animated Cartoons* (New York: Facts on File, 1991), 122, 133. See this work for more information.

19. Marchione, *Americans of Italian Heritage*, 201–207

20. Frank Sanello, *Stallone: A Rocky Life*, (Edinburgh and London: Mainstream Publishing, 1998); Emily Smith, *The Sylvester Stallone Handbook: Everything You Need to Know about Sylvester Stallone* (Tebbo, 2011).

21. 21 Gerard Peary, *Quentin Taratntino Interviews* (Jackson, Mississippi, University of Mississippi Press, 1998), 30.

22. Ben Lawton, "American Through Italian American Eyes: Dream or Nightmare," in *Italian Americans Celebrate Life, The Arts and Popular Culture*, eds. Paola A. Sensi Isolani and Anthony J. Tamburri (Staten Island, N.Y.:, The American Italian Historical Association, 1990), 59–78.

23. Karen Ward Mahar, *Women Filmmakers in Early Hollywood (Baltimore: Johns Hopkins University Press, 2006)*, 29–30. A study on the topic of women pioneers in the movie industry which cites two who were important in administrative capacities in Italy's cinema industry.

24. Gary Marshall, *Wake Me When it's Funny : How to Break into Show Business and Stay There* (New York:Newmarket Press, 1997); Lawrence Crown, *Penny Marshall, An UnAuthorized Biography* (Los Angeles: Renaissance Books, 1999).

25. James M. Welsh, Gene Philps, and Rodney F. Hill, *The Francis Ford Coppola Encyclopedia* (Lanham: Scarecrow Press, 2010), XVII.

26. Dotson Rader, "I Wouldn't Give Any Of It Back," *Parade*, May 4, 2004.

27. *Roanoke Times*, January 30, 2011.

28. See "The Confessions of Michael De Luca," *Hollywood Reporter*, February 24, 2011.

29. *New York Times*, April 27, 2001.

30. Bertellini, *Italy in Early American Cinema*, 179

31. David M. Fine, *Imagining Los Angeles: A City in Fiction* (Reno: University of Nevada Press, 2004), 182.

32. Biographical information can be found in John Fante, *Ask The Dust* (New York: HarperPerennial Modern Classics, 2006); John Fante, *The Road to Los Angeles* (Santa Rosa: Black Arrow Press, 2000); John Fante, *The John Fante Reader* ed. Stephen Cooper (New York: Harper Perennial, 2002).

33. *New York Times,* February 10, 1975.

34. Richard Alleva, "Renovations: 'Psycho,' 'You've Got Mail' & 'Prince of Egypt'," *Commonweal*, January, 1999.
35. *New York Times*, August 31, 2006.
36. Nicholas Pileggi, *Wiseguy* (New York: Pocket Books, 2010).
37. Jacqueline Reich, "Italian American Filmmakers: Nancy Savoca: In Appreciation," *Italian Americana* 13, no. 1 (Winter 1995): 11–15.
38. Jim Distasio, "He's So Money," *Fra Noi*, August 2011, 25–26.
39. *New York Times*, April 18, 2011.
40. Nick Pinkerton, "James DeMonaco's Debut, Staten Island, *Village Voice*, November 17, 2009.
41. Miller, *Kaleidoscopic Lens*, 93.

CHAPTER 6

WHAT'S IN A NAME?

NAME CHANGERS, NAME KEEPERS,
AND NAME ADOPTERS

From its beginnings, name changing has been a peculiar phenomenon of
the film industry. Convinced that Americans would be more at ease and
comfortable with "American sounding" names as opposed to those that
were in sharp contrast to the Anglo-Saxon model, the namechanging practice was in fact dictated by a pragmatic business calculation that linked
success in the movie industry to mass appeal. It must be remembered
that the rise of the movie industry coincided with intensified debate over
immigration. From the 1880s until the end of the 1920s, the nation rever-
berated with insistent demands to curb the immigration then increasingly
emanating from southern and eastern Europe, namely Italians, Greeks,
Poles, and Russian Jews, rather than from northern and western Europe
as had been the norm earlier. Immigration restriction finally became a
reality with the immigration quotas of the 1920s. Furthermore, the fact
that many of the emerging major studios were owned by immigrants
of Jewish background convinced movie moguls of the need to alter
names to present a more acceptable, even if more bland, appearance.
Accordingly, "moviemakers and moguls anglicized their own names and
those of their stars,"[1] The Wonskolaser brothers became Warner Brothers,

Schmuel Gelbfisz became Samuel Goldwyn and Lazar Meir became Louis Mayer. Actor and comedian Benjamin Kubelsky became Jack Benny, Isidore Iskowitz became Eddy Cantor, Archibald Leach became Cary Grant, Gwyllyn Samuel Newton Ford became Glenn Ford, and Bernard Schwartz became Tony Curtis, while among actresses, Marion Pauline Levy became Paulette Goddard, Frances Ethel Gumm became Judy Garland, and Margarita Carmen Cansino became Rita Hayworth. Simply put, "Producers followed the line of least resistance, they produced movies that offended the fewest and the weakest people."[2]

Not surprisingly, a number of Italian Americans in the film industry also changed their names or had their names changed for them, sometimes completely obliterating their ethnic background. One of the first examples in this regard was silent-screen actor Bull Montana, born Luigi Montagna in 1887 in Voghera, Italy. He came to this country with his family as a child and grew into maturity bearing a plug-ugly countenance replete with cauliflower ears and crooked teeth—the perfect background to enter the wrestling circuits of New York and New Jersey, near where he lived. Following initial success as a wrestler, he moved into the western part of the country and rechristened himself Bull Montana, enjoying a reputation as a top wrestler, who in one exhibition match wrestled with heavyweight boxing champion Jack Dempsey. Through a friendship with popular action actor Douglas Fairbanks, he moved into the movie industry, usually in supporting roles and often appearing as a gruesome villain as, for instance, in *Victory* (1919) which featured Lon Chaney, a great actor of that era. Among the major hits in which Montana had parts were *The Four Horsemen of the Apocalypse* (1921) and *Son of the Sheik* (1926), both of which starred Rudolph Valentino. Unlike many others, Montana was fortunate to be able to survive the radical change from silent to sound films, in which he continued to play bit parts, most notably in the *Flash Gordon* movie serials that began in 1936. He died in California in 1950 and was buried in Calvary Cemetery. Revealingly, his ugly countenance was cited as grounds for his divorce in 1931, as *Time*, a national magazine, wrote: "Mr. Montana admits his face frightens women and children. Mrs. Montana said she was afraid to live with him."[3]

Another early name-change example was Montague "Monte" Banks, whose 1897 birth name in Cesena, Italy was Mario Bianchi. Upon coming to the United States in 1914, he appeared in stage musicals using his original name, Bianchi, and worked as a comedian, a film director, and an actor during the silent-film era, in which he starred in films like *Play Safe* (1927) that featured a daring runaway train sequence. His unique screen persona baffled while it impressed the perceptive, Pulitzer Prize-winning critic Walter Kerr, who provided a helpful thumbnail sketch.

> It is almost impossible now to describe a once-popular comedian like Monte Banks by speaking of his mannerisms; he doesn't seem to have any. He is short, on the plump side, possessed of a miniature mustache that would seem suave on a head waiter but it is somehow a badge of apprehension on him. He is likeable. But, after a long and rigorous training at Warner Brothers and elsewhere, when he came to make features independently he took refuge in "thrill" comedies that owed a great deal to Harold Lloyd. Let it be said that he made these legitimately: in Play Safe he lowers himself by a rope from the roof of a runaway train toward the open door of a boxcar, letting the girl climb first on him and then up the rope while he sways precariously over embankments, bridges, and mountainside drops that are unmistakably authentic. The stunting is impeccable, worth keeping in film anthologies; but we cannot quite remember the man.[4]

His talents notwithstanding, the advent of talking pictures found him at a disadvantage in acting parts because of his heavy accent, thereby leading to his decision to move to England in 1928, where he married popular musical-comedy star Gracie Fields, whom he directed in several films. He then returned to Hollywood, where he directed *Great Guns* (1941) a Laurel and Hardy film that was not well received. Now calling himself William Montague, he also played a supporting role in *Blood and Sand*

(1940), which featured Tyrone Power. At the time of his death in Italy in 1950, Banks was an executive with Twentieth-Century Fox.

Terence Hill, who was born Mario Girotti in Venice, Italy in 1939 and who had an Italian father and a German mother, was one of three children. The family moved while he was a child to a town near Dresden, Germany —the excessively firebombed city—in which the family survived the Second World War and which was the place where he grew up and learned to speak German fluently. He was not allowed to forget his Italian roots, however, as his father read to him, in Italian, *The Little Flowers of Saint Francis of Assisi* and *Saint Francis of Assisi's The Canticle of the Creatures* to teach him both Italian and values such as love and peace. The family subsequently moved back to Italy, where he became active in physical sports like gymnastics and swimming, while also beginning his acting career by attending the Actors School in Rome. He soon teamed up with Italian swimming-champion Carlo Pedersoli and together the two athletically-inclined actors proceeded to perform all their own stunts while making dozens of spaghetti westerns in Italy. *Trinity is My Name* (1970) and *Trinity is Still My Name* (1971), both slapstick western comedies, are among the more popular films of this genre. Mario also made a number of films in Germany. Both Mario and Carlo were persuaded to anglicize their names. Thus Mario Girotti became Terrence Hill. He apparently chose the name as a lark—he was supposedly given twenty names from which to choose before deciding on his screen moniker. Meanwhile Carlo Pedersoli became Bud Spencer.

In 1971, after Terence and his family moved to the United States, making a home for themselves in Massachusetts, he began to make American films, including *Mr. Billion* (1977) and *March or Die* (1977). When he could find no other producers for his project of filming a contemporary version of *Don Camillo*, he decided to assume the roles of producer, director, and lead role-player in the film. He subsequently directed other films. In more recent years, Terence has divided his time between the United States and a small town in Italy to star as a wise and understanding priest who solves crimes in *Don Matteo*, a television series that enjoyed success in Italy and other countries, including the United States. He also continues making American movies, the latest being *Doc West* (2009). Hill is married and is the father of three children, one of whom died in an automobile accident.[5]

Handsome Guy Williams, born in New York City in 1924 as Armand Joseph Catalano, the son of Attilio and Clare Catalano, had hazel eyes and a height of six foot three that led first to a career as a fashion model and then a career as an actor. Nicknamed Armando, he grew up in an Italian neighborhood in Brooklyn where he went to public school, started but did not continue higher education, and worked in various capacities during the Second World War including a welder, cost accountant, aircraft-parts inspector, and a fashion model. As a result of the latter job, his face was featured in popular magazines, which consequently proved pivotal to his decision to change his name to Guy Williams. Determined to become an actor, in 1946 he went to Hollywood, signed a contract with MGM and appeared in a few films such as *The Beginning or the End* (1947). He signed a contract with Universal Studios and was cast in supporting roles in several films including *Bonzo Goes to College* (1952) and *The Golden Blade* (1953). Although he never quite reached the pinnacle of movie stardom, he continued to act in television, where he signed a contract with Walt Disney to play the swashbuckling hero Zorro, on the condition he grow a modest mustache and learn how to fence and play a guitar. The *Zorro* series, which became an instant hit, ran for two years, generated two movies, and paid Williams handsomely.

Subsequently, Guy Williams's cinematic career found him making a few movies in Europe while periodically playing in various television shows, such as *Bonanza* and *Lost in Space*. In the 1970s, he moved to Argentina where, because of his *Zorro* films, he enjoyed such popularity that he had become a pop hero. Financially well off, he decided to retire in Argentina where he lived for the rest of his life. He was married to Janice Cooper and had two children: Guy Steven Catalano and Toni Catalano.

Years after his death in 1989, the name of Guy Williams lives on a website of Zorro devotees.[6]

Captivating, catchy, and easy to remember names with show business pizzazz were virtually a requirement for entertainment field aspirants. That consideration may well have been the reason why Catherine Gloria Balotta, who was born in Cleveland, Ohio in 1925, the daughter of an Italian immigrant and raised in a genuine, Catholic, Italian American household, became Kaye Ballard. As she put it: "My parents were extremely traditional Italians whose marriage had been arranged. Even so, the union lasted nearly six decades."[7]

By the time she was five years old, Kaye evinced a desire to perform both at home and at school, where she was known for her antics and where she honed the art of impersonating her favorite entertainers. With encouragement from her father and grandmother but not from her mother, who expected her to learn to cook, clean, and get married, she made her stage debut at age fifteen in *Stage Door Canteen* in Cleveland, and her Broadway debut in 1946 in *Three to Make Ready*. She tried different show business names, including Kay Ballad (as in song) before settling on Kaye Ballard. She performed in Cleveland nightclubs, burlesque, and vaudeville and toured with the Spike Jones Orchestra as a vocalist, thereby becoming one of the nation's most appealing singers, presaging her evolution into an established and versatile entertainer who not only performed strikingly as a singer but also as a surprisingly successful comedienne and actress. In explaining her ability to transform herself when cast into the role of Molly Goldberg, the quintessential Jewish mother, Kaye stated, "From food to guilt and back to food again, the cultural similarities between Jewish and Italian families have always amazed me. Maybe that's why I always been so comfortable playing Jewish mothers."[8] Kaye then branched out into stage plays and television, where she was frequently typecast as an outspoken, loud-mouthed and, for the most part, Italian character actress. Her Hollywood films include *A House is Not a Home* (1964), *Joey Takes a Cab* (1991), and *Ava's Magical Adventure*

(1994). Never married but with remarkable staying power, Kaye Ballard (Catherine Bilotta) has performed professionally for over seven decades.

Although the family originally lived in Brooklyn, Connie Francis (Concetta Rosa Maria Franconero) was born in the Italian Ironbound neighborhood of Newark, New Jersey in 1938, where her grandparents and many relatives lived. She attended public schools in Newark until the family moved to Belleville, New Jersey where she graduated as class salutatorian from Belleville High School. As a three-year old child, she showed an inclination to music and took up accordion lessons from her accordion-playing father and also began to perform on stage as a singer, a useful background that led to her appearance in a New York City television show for talented child singers and performers hosted by Arthur Godfrey, then television's master commercial pitchman. It was Godfrey who, though duly impressed by her singing of "Daddy's Little Girl," nevertheless had such difficulty pronouncing her name that he recommended she change it to something "easy and Irish." She recalled Godfrey saying

> "Little girl, come over here with your accordion. How do you pronounce your name again?" And I said, as if speaking a foreign language "Franc-o-nero." He whistled and said, "That's a toughie. Why don't we give you a nice, easy to pronounce old Irish name like, let's see, Francis." I said "Oh, Mr. Godfrey, please, please let me be Connie Franconero just for tonight. My father will have a fit." So, he struggled through it and said Connie Franconero, which incidentally, my name has never been legally changed. After that, my father said "Yeah, Connie Francis. That has a nice sound to it. That's not too bad. We'll use that."[9]

Using the name Francis, she sang weekly for four years but seemed to have difficulty succeeding to the next level of the entertainment world. As a consequence of show business disappointment, she was on the verge of accepting a pre-med scholarship at New York University when her father suggested she record a new arrangement of an old song, "Who's Sorry Now," that crystallized so marvelously that Dick Clark felt compelled to play it regularly on his famous *American Bandstand* program, while he hailed her as "a new girl singer that is heading straight for the number one spot." Such was the beginning of a enormous singing career that saw her records reign among the top sellers—over one hundred of her records sold in the course of her career in the United States and abroad. She also sang ballads in Italian, developing an enthusiastic following with her tearful and emotive rendition of a sentimental favorite, "Mama," which, interestingly, she was initially hesitant to sing on *The Perry Como Show* for fear of being labeled an ethnic singer; yet it turned out to be one of her biggest hits, one that she performed in many languages. One source described the deep impact it had on Elvis Presley who, watching her singing the song during a concert just after he had lost his own mother, became so overcome with emotion that he had to leave the theater. Although Connie did not at first speak the Italian language, being familiar only with her grandmother's dialect version, she did recall the melodies: "I just remembered songs my grandmother taught me, and songs that I learned for the recordings." She also hired an Italian tutor.[10]

Enjoying great popularity in the 1960s, Connie made several Hollywood films, including *Where The Boys Are* (1960), *Follow The Boys* (1963), *Looking For Love* (1964), and *When the Boys Meet The Girls* (1965). Unfortunately, her triumphant professional career was not matched by good fortune in her private life—particularly in choosing a husband. She dearly loved her singing peer, the talented but arrogant Bobby Darin, but due to the opposition of her overprotective father, never married him; marrying and divorcing four times instead.[11] In addition, she suffered the trauma of rape at a location where she was scheduled to perform, lost her brother, who was murdered, required debilitating nasal surgery and, at the insistence of her controlling father, underwent psychiatric treatment for long periods. In her later years she resumed her career, singing at concerts and appearing at nostalgic events like her return to Newark, New Jersey in May 2010 to make a new recording of "Who's Sorry Now" on the fiftieth anniversary of the movie of the same name, in which she starred. Reminiscing about her checkered life, she says she would like to be remembered

> not for the heights I've reached, but for the depth from which I've risen. There are a lot of people who have had my success in this business. There were exhilarating highs and abysmal lows. But, it was fighting to get out of those lows that I feel most proud of.

Although little about the name Bruno Kirby indicates his Italian ancestry, he was, in fact, born in 1946 as Giovanni Quidaciolu, Jr., the son of the actor known as Bruce Kirby. Bruno went to local schools and grew up in the Hell's Kitchen section of New York City, where he also took lessons in singing and dancing, before moving with his family to California, where he launched his acting career by appearing in television shows, often as an assertive, pushy, streetwise character with a highly distinctive, scratchy, tenor voice. It was exactly that image that landed him a major movie part alongside Robert De Niro as Clemenza, a role that required speaking mostly in Italian in *The Godfather Part II* (1974). Bruno continued acting in such highly regarded television shows as *It's Garry Shandling's Show*, as well as a number of movies, most notably in *When Harry Met Sally* (1989) and *City Slickers* (1991), in which he teamed up with Billy Crystal. Married to actress Lynn Sellers in 2006, he was diagnosed with leukemia that led to his death in that year.[12]

Because the Italian ancestry of some actors is derived from their mothers, they are known by the non-Italian names of their fathers. This is the case in two examples that will be briefly reviewed: Tim Van Patten and Vin Diesel. Timothy was born into a Brooklyn theatrical family in 1959 to Richard Van Patten, of Dutch heritage, and Eleanor Delligati, of Italian lineage. The half brother of actors Dick and Joyce Van Patten, he grew up in Massapequa, Long Island, where he attended local schools as he prepared to enter the acting field. He made progress in his career, appearing in television shows and making his impressive film debut as the leader of a drug gang in *Class of 1984* (1982). While continuing to perform in television and movies, he also became involved in other aspects of the industry, such as writing screenplays, directing and producing. Made-for-television shows and episodes in series like *The Sopranos, Sex and the City, The Pacific War,* and *Broadway Empire* are among his more successful directing accomplishments.

Vin Diesel, who, according to various sources, is the son of a Black man and an Italian mother, describes himself as a multicultural actor, one who is not given parts to portray an African American because of his light-skinned pigmentation, nor given traditional White roles because he is not deemed white enough. However, he has acted in Italian American roles as, for example, Pvt. Adrian Caparzo, an Italian American soldier, in *Saving Private Ryan* (1998) and Chris Varick, an Italian American broker in *Boiler Room* (2000). He grew up and attended school in Greenwich Village, New York, earning some money after school by working as a bouncer, trading on his muscular figure and physical strength. Sporting a bald head, he entered the acting field and gained experience in off-Broadway roles before launching a filmmaking career that has catapulted him to the point where he enjoys considerable success in making fast-paced action films. Vin Diesel has also been effective as a writer, director and producer, assuming all these roles plus the starring acting part in his independent movie *The Strays* (1997), a drama in which he played a drug dealer and a hustler. It is a low budget movie that, while not a commercial success, so impressed influential theater people that it opened many doors for him in the movie industry.

Because the names of the actors covered above retained nothing reminiscent of an Italian origin, they could be said to have followed the script of the early movie moguls who promoted the concept of obliterating any name that sounded foreign. It cannot be said, however that Montana, Banks, Hill, Williams, Ballard, Francis, Van Patten and Diesel completely abandoned their ethnic roots, since any scrutiny beyond the surface reveals an ongoing Italian identification. Montana frequently referred to himself as the Italian wrestling champion, while with Banks his Italian identity was evident in his occasional return to his birth name, and Hill's Italian-language films and character portrayals show a strong Italian identity. Notice must be taken, too, of the name Catalano, which is carried by Guy Williams' children, and that the Kaye Ballard's Italian ethnic portrayals easily place her within the ethnic group. Connie Francis has never legally forfeited her name of Franconero. Van Patten and Diesel call attention to their Italian backgrounds in biographical sketches. Other Hollywood personalities who changed their original Italian names to nonethnic ones include Nicholas Cage (Nicholas Coppola) , Harry Warren (Salvatore Guaragna), Carol Lawrence (Carolina Maria Laraia), Connie Stevens (Concetta Ingoglia), Robert Blake (Michael Gubitosi), and Hulk Hogan (Terry Gene Bollea).

Mention should be made of those actors of Italian descent who changed their names for show business purposes, but whose adopted names retained their Italianness. They include, among others, Rudolph Valentino (Rodolfo Alfonso Raffaello Piero Filiberto Guglielmi di Valentina d'Antonguolla), Don Ameche, Robert Alda, Lou Costello (Louis Francis Cristillo), Vic Damone (Vito Farinola), Mario Lanza (Alfred Arnold Cocozza), Anthony Franciosa (Giovanni Tomaso Tedesco), Jack Scalia, and Bobby Darin (Walden Robert Cassotto). We will review this phenomenon in more detail in the lives of Don Ameche, Robert Alda and Anthony Franciosa.

Don Ameche was born Dominic Felix Amici in Kenosha, Wisconsin. His mother was of Irish and German background while his father, Felix, was an Italian immigrant whose last name was Amici. The Amici clan, which settled in Wisconsin, included Don's brother James, who became a nationally known radio announcer, and a cousin, Alan Ameche, who became nationally famous after winning the Heisman Trophy, in 1954, playing football at the University of Wisconsin. At age eleven, Don attended St. Berchman's Academy in Marion, Wisconsin, a Catholic boarding school for boys run by the Sisters of Mercy, where he was known as wild, yet where he also excelled academically, receiving medals for drama and elocution, while also playing in the orchestra and acting in leading roles in school plays. Don spent two years at Columbia College (the forerunner of Loras College) before attending Marquette University and a couple of other institutions of higher learning, where he studied law until he decided on an acting career. During his long career he played vaudeville, performed on the legitimate stage, and was on the radio until he began acting in motion pictures in the mid 1930s. Within a few years he became an established Hollywood star, appearing in numerous films over nearly six decades. His casting as Alexander Graham Bell in *The Story of Alexander Graham Bell* (1939) rendered him a virtual household byword as people joked about Ameche as the inventor of the telephone. He was regarded as a proper, old-school actor, one who at one point demurred when the script called for him to use the "f-word" agreeing to continue only after he apologized to everyone on the set for being compelled to use such a harsh vulgarity in his or her presence. A versatile actor who appeared in musicals, comedies and more serious roles, he won an Oscar for Best Supporting Actor for his work in the movie *Cocoon* (1985). Married to Honore Prendergast from 1932 until her death in 1986, the Ameches had six children. Don Ameche died in 1993 at the age of eighty-five. He was cremated and his ashes are buried at St. Philomena's Cemetery, in Asbury, Iowa.[13]

Robert Alda, born in New York City in 1914 as Alphonso Giovanni Roberto D'Abruzzo (the blending of two names resulted in Alda), was the son of Frances and Anthony D'Abruzzo, a barber. He graduated from Stuyvesant High School before entering the world of entertainment. He played in vaudeville as a singer and dancer prior to receiving roles in films. His early films included *Rhapsody in Blue* (1945), in which he played George Gershwin; *Cloak and Dagger* (1946), in which he was cast as Pinkie, a no-nonsense American who leads Italian guerrilla fighters; and *Imitation of Life* (1959), a melodrama in which he plays Allen Loomis, a theatrical agent. He also had roles in a number of Italian-made films and television shows and was equally successful in Broadway shows, including *Guys and Dolls,* which earned him a Tony Award. Joan Brown, winner of the Miss New York beauty pageant ,was Alda's first wife, and the mother of actor Alan Alda. His second wife, with whom he remained married until his death in 1986, was Flora Martino. His son Alan Alda became even more famous as an actor in movies and television. Interestingly, Robert Alda sought to discourage his son from acting.

> My father did not want me to be a actor. He was an actor. He wanted me to be a doctor because that's what he always wanted to be. Nevertheless he brought me onstage when I was six months old. He was working burlesque and he brought me, as a joke to the other actors. And I was on stage with him for various times throughout my childhood—he still tried to talk me out of becoming an actor. And I did the same thing with my children. I tried to talk them out of becoming actresses, but then I wrote parts for them in movies. It's a generic quirk in my family.

Another example of name changing that remained within the ethnic matrix is that of Tony Franciosa, who was born to parents of Italian ancestry as Anthony George Papaleo. Following the breakup of his parents' marriage when he was one year old, Anthony was brought up by his mother and understandably adopted her last name: Franciosa. After working odd jobs and sometimes sleeping in flophouses, when eighteen he attended an audition for actors at the YMCA and was chosen for two plays. He was a member of the Actors Studio and associated with a rising generation of Italian Americans, including Ben Gazzara and Harry Guardino, which was making its way into filmdom at the time. Franciosa then began to make movies, frequently playing moody, troubled and complicated young men in such films as, *A Face in the Crowd* (1957), *Wild Is the Wind* (1957), *The Long Hot Summer* (1958), *The Naked Maja* (1958), *The Story on Page One* (1959), *Period of Adjustment* (1962), *Rio Conchos* (1964), and *The Pleasure Seekers* (1964).

Franciosa possessed a pugnacious temperament that got him into trouble in Hollywood, where he reputedly had fiery disputes with directors and nasty outbursts with other actors; he even drew a brief jail term for punching a press photographer. He later confessed, "I wasn't quite mature enough psychologically and emotionally for it.[14] His combativeness turned people off in the movie capital, forcing him to make films elsewhere, as well as looking for acting roles on television. He was married four times—once to Shelly Winters—and had three children who survived him when he died, in 2006, at age seventy-seven.

Born in the Italian Hospital of the tough Lower East Side neighborhood of New York City in 1930, Ben Gazzara (Biagio Anthony) was the son of immigrants: Angela Cusumano, his mother, and Antonio, his father, who never learned English. There was an older brother who served as a soldier in World War II. Like all Italian Americans in his neighborhood, Ben followed the careers of Joe DiMaggio in baseball and Rocky Graziano in boxing. His description of the neighborhood's reaction to Graziano's motorcade in 1947, following Rocky's achievement in becoming the World's Middleweight Champion, is revealing:

> When he came up my block, sitting on the top of the backseat of a convertible, you'd think he was a king or a president. We went crazy. Rocky made us proud. I hoped that someday I, too, would make people proud.[15]

Although Ben describes his parents as loving people, there was a generational gap—his mother was forty-five years old when she gave birth to him and his father continually yearned to go back to Sicily. As a young boy, Ben led a lonely life, served as an altar boy, and, for a time, attended St. Simon Stock High School in the Bronx.[16] He then decided to go into acting by attending The Actors Studio and made his film debut in *Anatomy of Murder* (1959), an early Hollywood vehicle which addressed sex and rape in graphic terms and which has been rated as one of the twelve best trial films of all time. He also had featured roles in *The Young Doctors* (1961), *A Rage to Live* (1965), *The Bridge at Remagen* (1969), *Husbands* (1970), *Capone* (1975), *Voyage of the Damned* (1976), and *High Velocity* (1976).

Gazzara found considerable work on television, both as an actor and director. He faced various adversities in his life, including depression, the death of his best friend, John Cassavetes, and throat cancer. He has been married three times and credits his third wife, Elke, with saving him psychologically and spiritually. He lives with her in their home in Italy.[17]

It has been observed that in the last third of the twentieth century the name-changing phenomenon, so characteristic of Hollywood, began to diminish, as actors became more come comfortable with, and readily used, their birth names, for example, Barbra (Barbara) Streisand, George Segal, and Dustin Hoffman. Similarly, Italian Americans with distinctive ethnic names became increasingly common in Hollywood, for example, the actors Al Pacino, Robert De Niro, John Travolta, Sylvester Stallone, Paul Sorvino, and Leonardo Di Caprio, and the directors Francis Ford Coppola, Martin Scorsese and Quentin Tarantino. One can only imagine how Hollywood would have tinkered with these appellations in an earlier period. It is instructive to know that some actors of an earlier generation did indeed reject the suggestion to change their names—Frank Sinatra is a prime case in point.

Just prior to Frank Sinatra becoming the premier male singer in the nation and embarking on a career that would lead to Hollywood stardom, he attracted the attention of popular bandleader Harry James, who signed him on as the band's vocalist. When James suggested that Sinatra change his name to the less Italian-sounding Frankie Satin, the Hoboken singer adamantly rejected the notion: "I said no way baby, My name is Sinatra, Frank fucking Sinatra."[18]

Endnotes

1. Miller, *Kaleidoscopic Lens*, 5.
2. Miller, *Kaleidoscopic Lens*, 5.
3. *Time*, August 31, 1931.
4. Walter Kerr, *The Silent Clowns* (New York: Da Capo Press, 1990).
5. "Candida Martinelli's Italophile Site," accessed September 1, 2011, http://italophiles.com/.
6. Antoinette Girgenti Lane, *Man Behind the Mask* (Boalsburg, Pennsylvania: BearManor Media, 2005).
7. Kaye Ballard and Jim Hessleman, *How I Lost Ten Pounds in 53 Years* (New York: Watson-Guptill Publications, 2006), 8. See also Otto Bruno, "Storied, Yet Unsung," *Fra Noi*, May 2011, 36–39.
8. Ballard, *How I Lost Ten*, 9.
9. Connie Francis, *Who's Sorry Now* (New York: St. Martin's Press, 1984), 35.
10. Francis, *Who's Sorry Now*.
11. James Roberts Parish, *Hollywood Songsters, Singers Who Act and Actors Who Sing* (New York: Routledge, 2003), 217.
12. *New York Times*, August 17, 2006.
13. Ben Ohmart, *Don Ameche, The Kenosha Comeback Kid* (Albany, Georgia: BearManor Media, 2007).
14. Hollywood," *USA Today*, January 20, 2006.
15. Gazzara, *In The Moment*, 43.
16. Gazzara, *In The Moment*, 15–26.
17. Otto Bruno, "The Path Less Traveled," *Fra Noi*, August 2011, 36–39.
18. Hamill, *Why Sinatra Matters*, 38.

CHAPTER 7

CUISINE, COMEDY, AND CHARACTER ACTORS

CUISINE

The role of food as a central motif in film harks back to the era of silent movies, when it was used in a variety of ways: for all-out comedy, to caricature immigrant groups, or as a familiar means of communicating a movie plot. In a word, food conveys a universal experience to which audiences readily relate; it acts as a metaphor for the complexities of culture. Food, family and warm fraternal feeling surrounding the kitchen or dining room table are synonymous with Italian life, so essential that no matter how impoverished Italian immigrants were, they would make astonishing efforts to provide a wholesome, substantial, and frequently stupendously memorable meal. Sundays were sacrosanct occasions; they were the time when the family gathered together, and there was always room for one more at the table. It was in this familial setting where family members not only enjoyed gustatory treats, but where they also learned about Italian traditions.

This abiding feature of their heritage formed a major part their cultural baggage, an inheritance brought over to this country and perpetuated by Italian Americans of the first and second generations. Though succeeding generations have abandoned much of their tradition, they still pay homage, even if attenuated, to this custom. Accordingly, here in the United States, Italian food has had its most visible and deepest influence; it became more and more recognizable and went beyond spaghetti and meatballs as Americans became better acquainted with readily available, authentic ingredients. Not surprisingly, this cultural characteristic appears as a significant feature in many movies in which Italian American family life is portrayed and can be seen in films like *House of Strangers* (1949), *Love With The Proper Stranger* (1963), and *Moonstruck* (1987), among others, while opulent films like *The Leopard* (1963) reveal a similar centrality of food in Italian life. The popularity of Italian food is acknowledged; Italian cuisine is near the top of the list of foods enjoyed by Americans as a whole; it is so pervasive that it prompted play writer Neil Simon to state, "There are two laws in the universe: the law of gravity, and everyone likes Italian food."[1] Confirmation of this truth is further demonstrated in the 2011 publication *How Italian Food Conquered the World,* which has elicited great interest, with one reviewer suggesting that the title should be amended to "Italian American food conquers the World."[2] Many scenes in Mafia films like *The Godfather* take place in restaurants and around tables, where significant events occur while characters are eating. In one memorable scene, Michael Corleone (Al Pacino) asserts his grab for mobster power as he sits at a table in Louis' Italian American Restaurant in the Bronx, where he shoots a corrupt police captain while the man is chewing on "the best veal in the city." The uniqueness of Italian food is so evident that it is noted for its absence, as in *Godfather Part II,* in which traditional food is notably missing as Michael Corleone (again played by Al Pacino) attempts to americanize his son's communion party with non-Italian food and music. Seeing through the chimera, Frank Pentangeli (Michael V. Gazzo) rejects an offer of canapés, demanding; "bring out the peppers and sausage," while complaining about the absence of Italian melodies. There is a rare respite from violence in *Goodfellas* (1990) during a kitchen scene that finds director Martin Scorsese's real-life mother playing a character preoccupied with how to best prepare food, specifically how to shave slivers of garlic into puttanesca sauce, while completely oblivious to the prevailing viciousness of the setting.

The movie *Fatso* (1980), a somewhat sad comedy, is an exceptional cinematic example that depicts the part food played in the lives of Italian Americans. Significantly, the film was written and directed by Italian American Anne Bancroft, who also starred in the movie as Antoinette, the sister of Dom DeLuise, who was cast in the role of rotund Dominic. Dominic is constantly confronted with the challenge of denying his lifelong love affair with food if he is to win his sweetheart Lydia. Accordingly, he joins a high-voltage, crash, weight-reducing program requiring heroic measures to resist his natural temptation to enjoy food. He makes these efforts only to fail and, dismayed, he reacts by going on a gigantic food binge, eating every edible morsel he can seize. As the compulsively eating protagonist, Dom manages to create both comedy and pathos as his character, Dominic, happily learns that Lydia loves him because of who he is and in spite of his weight. Absorbed in his courtship of Lydia, he discovers a love that is more intense than his love of food.

A close DeLuise family friend and a fellow Italian American, Anne Bancroft was inspired to write the film script for *Fatso* after spending the afternoon in the DeLuise kitchen following the funeral of Dom's father (who had worked in the Department of Sanitation), where Dom and his sister Antoinette related the story of Dom's food obsession and its impact on his life. The film accurately depicts Dom's struggle with obesity. The two main characters are authentically named Dominic and Antoinette, while original DeLuise family photos were used in the set decoration and bit parts were given to Dom's mother and aunt, who appear in the film sitting in front of a store and crocheting.

Born in Brooklyn, to Vincenza De Stefano and John DeLuise, Italian immigrants from the Basilicata region of Italy, Dom worshiped with his family in the Catholic Church directly across the street from their home. That church was Regina Pacis, a massive faux-Italian Renaissance structure with a high limestone bell tower and a wonderful shrine of the Blessed Mother which was the pride of Bensonhurst's Italians.[3] Dom attended P.S. 187 and McKinley Junior High School in Brooklyn, where a caring teacher recognized his talent and arranged an audition for him to attend the Manhattan High School of Performing Arts. He later went to Tufts University and then became an actor, comedian, director, television producer, chef, and author, frequently playing portly, lovable, butterball comedian roles. His comic genius found its way into many entertainment venues: stage plays, television, and movies. Food was a genuine passion in Dom DeLuise's life and accordingly obesity became a chronic, real-life problem; he reportedly weighed 325 pounds at one point. He was once quoted as saying,

> When I was a kid, if I had a fever, had a cold, had a fight, had a fall, had a cut, was depressed, had a disappointment, fell off a truck, woke up with a headache...no matter what the situation, my mother's solution was always, "Eat this. It'll make you feel better. "

Not surprisingly, he became a respected chef and authored two cookbooks: *Eat This, It'll Make You Feel Better* and *Eat This Too,* in which he demonstrated his favorite Italian recipes. He was married to actress Carol Arthur (Carol Arata) and at the time of his death, in 2009, had three sons who were involved in the movie business: Peter is a director and Michael and David are actors.[4]

Arguably, *Big Night* (1996) directed by Stanley Tucci, who also cowrote the screenplay with his cousin Joseph Tropiano, is the standout movie linking the love of food and Italian Americans. The film revolves around two immigrant brothers from Abruzzo, Primo (Tony Shalhoub) and Secondo (Stanley Tucci), who are trying to become successful restaurateurs offering authentic Italian food to Americans of the 1950s, patrons whose notion of Italian food barely strayed beyond spaghetti and meatballs. *The Big Night* is a drama pitting integrity against compromise, with the two brothers representing two kinds of skills: Primo that of a culinary artist while Secondo epitomizes business practicality. A complete restaurant film, much of the activity is divided between the kitchen and the dining room. Notwithstanding Secondo and Primo's efforts to provide customers with peerless, magnificent, and authentic food, their restaurant is failing—shockingly, people seem to prefer the uninspired, spaghetti-and-meatballs food of their competitor, Pascal. Primo and Secondo failed to obtain a loan from Pascal who, in rejecting the idea, proposes instead that they come to work for him, while also promising to bring popular bandleader Louis Prima to the brothers' restaurant. Primo and Secondo refuse Pascal's offer in the belief that they can, in fact, make a success of their restaurant once word gets out that Louis Prima dined in their establishment. And so ,hoping that Prima's visit that will revitalize their enterprise, they pour their last bit of savings into preparing the greatest banquet possible, inviting journalists and other guests to the big night in order to present a grand, spectacular, and colossal culinary masterpiece. The cooking scenes in the kitchen are so realistically conveyed that one reviewer says it prompts viewers to want to go out to an Italian restaurant right after the movie. Only when the big night comes and goes without an appearance by Louis Prima do they realize that they have been tricked by Pascal.

But the motivation for Big Night derived not merely from an interest in portraying Italian culinary creativeness. Tucci and his cousin Joseph Tropiano were desirous of creating "a movie in which Italians are depicted not as clichéd spaghetti-serving sentimentalists, nor as murderous back-stabbing Mafiosi, but as the complex, difficult, funny, stubborn, wonderful people they are."[5]

The film propelled Stanley Tucci into stardom; he won the New York Film Critics Award for Best Director, won the Best First Screenplay Independent Spirit Award and earned a nomination for an Oscar. Tucci, who was born in Peekskill, New York, to his father, a teacher and his mother, Joan (née Tropiano), a former secretary and writer, became one of several family members attracted to the field of acting. As a high school student, Stanley performed in plays along with Campbell Scott, son of actor George C. Scott, and then began to appear in Broadway shows and, subsequently in films and television dramas. His sister is actress Christine Tucci, and his cousin is screenwriter Joseph Tropiano, with whom he collaborated in *Big Night*. Together with Steve Buscemi, he runs a film production company and continues to have an interest in theater. A widower who lost his wife to cancer in 2009, he lives with his three children in Westchester County.[6]

COMEDY

The comedic strain in Italian and Italian American entertainment is longstanding, hearkening to the early period of mass Italian immigration that saw the ethnic community enjoying the performances of many comedians who made their living making people laugh. In time, Italian American comedians began to appear in movies, and though they did not abound in the same quantity as other ethnic groups, such as Jewish Americans, they did make their impact in Hollywood. In some instances, their Italianness would be palpable, while in others, it was not so noticeable. Among those Italian Americans who amused movie audiences were Jimmy Durante, Louis Prima, Jerry Colonna, Lou Costello, Dean Martin, Dom DeLuise, Kaye Ballard, Joy Behar, and Floyd Vivino. Having already discussed the careers of Martin and DeLuise at length, we will focus on a few others.

Born in Brooklyn, New York in 1893, Jimmy Durante was the third of four children born to Bartolomeo Durante, an immigrant from Salerno (1849–1942) and Rosa (Lentino) Durante (1858–1921). The Durante family lived in the rear rooms of Jimmy's father's barbershop and Jimmy, along with his brothers, occasionally lathered customers waiting to be shaved.[7] As a youngster, Jimmy served as an altar boy at St. Malachy's Roman Catholic Church in Manhattan (the Actor's Chapel), beginning a lifelong attachment as a faithful Catholic—it was said that when he lived in Las Vegas he could be seen outside of the Guardian Angel Cathedral after Sunday Mass, together with the priest, greeting people after the service was over. Jimmy's parents paid for his piano lessons, hoping he would take to classical music, however, Jimmy, influenced by Scott Joplin's music, turned instead to ragtime. In the eighth grade, Jimmy quit school and soon ventured into show business as a ragtime piano player, joining up with a New Orleans Jazz Ragtime band, where he developed his trademark style of interrupting his singing to deliver humorous lines. The places in which he performed during the 1910s and 1920s were regarded as shadowy speakeasies, unsavory surroundings since jazz halls were frequently linked with brothels in the New Orleans of the Roaring Twenties. While many clubs in which he performed were of dubious reputation, Jimmy led a life of relative rectitude. Moreover, his comedic sketches did not rely on off-color jokes. He also collaborated with African American songwriter Chris Smith in composing several songs, including "Daddy, Your Mama is Lonesome for You."

By the 1920s, Jimmy had become a recognized vaudeville star performing as part of the Clayton, Jackson and Durante trio. He also wrote his own musical compositions, like "Inka Dinka Doo," which became his signature song throughout a flourishing career. He appeared in comedic roles in Broadway stage musicals, radio, motion pictures and television shows. He worked in a number of Hollywood animated works, including singing the lead song in *Frosty the Snowman* (1969) which is shown repeatedly at Christmastime. Imitations of Durante's raspy voice appeared in other animated works; some *Looney Tunes* cartoons were made based on his character. Movie audiences became familiar with cartoons that used many of his lines, like, "dat's my boy" and "I got a million of 'em!"

Known to friends, family, and fans as The Schnozzola because of his Cyrano-sized nose, he endeared himself to millions of people by mangling the English language. Durante became one of the nation's most lovable and most imitated comedians with his fractured use of language, including "dat's moral turpentine!,", "It's a catastastroke!" (for catastrophe), "Everybody wants ta get inta the act!," "Umbriago!," and "Ha-cha-cha-chaaaaaaa!" Durante recorded an album of popular tunes, *September Song,* that became a bestseller and helped to introduce him to another generation of moviegoers years after his passing—especially his singing of "As Time Goes By" in the opening scene of *Sleepless in Seattle* (1993), followed by "Make Someone Happy" at the film's end.

Jimmy's truly remarkable film career found him appearing in many musical and comedic movies, commencing with *Roadhouse Nights* (1930), and including *Palooka* (1934); in which he sings the song he wrote, "Inka Dinka Doo;" and *Red, Hot and Blue* (1936). He last movie was the popular comedy *It's a Mad Mad Mad Mad World* (1963). Jimmy, who had one of the most popular television shows in the 1950s, always ended his programs with the line, "Goodnight Mrs. Calabash, wherever you are," engendering much speculation as to who Mrs. Calabash was. In reality, he spoke the line in remembrance of his first wife, Jeanne Olsen, whom he married in 1921 in St. Malachy's Church and who had shown a liking for a small town they once stopped in called Calabas. She died in 1943 and was continually remembered by Jimmy. In 1960, he married his second wife, Margaret "Margie" Little, and together the couple adopted a baby, Cecilia Alicia (CeCe Durante-Bloum). Jimmy was known for his generosity, giving lavishly to The Fraternal Order of Eagles, an organization that raised funds for abused and handicapped children; Jimmy Durante Children's Fund was named in his honor for raising over twenty million dollars.[8]

Gerardo Luigi "Jerry" Colonna, son of Italian immigrant parents, was born in Boston in 1904. His distinctive facial features—large popping eyes and huge handlebar mustache worn in emulation of his grandfather's enormous moustache—rendered him a recognizable figure on the screen. He possessed a musical inclination, working a job as a longshoreman by day to finance his music studies. Colonna was an extremely gifted jazz musician who played drums but truly excelled as a trombonist; at one time he was considered one of the five best trombonists in the country and made a record of Dixieland-style music. Accordingly, he obtained jobs playing trombone with leading bands that frequently played for radio shows in the 1930s and 1940s. Colonna was also a songwriter, whose credits include "At Dusk," "I Came to Say Goodbye," "Sleighbells in the Sky," and "Take Your Time."

He loved to play pranks, including a ruse that tricked famous comedian Fred Allen who, apprised that an Italian singer, named Giovanni "Jerry" Colonna (an imposter), sought an appointment, mistook him for an up and coming opera tenor and agreed to give him an audition. When Fred heard Jerry's earsplitting singing, he literally fell to the floor in laughter and offered him guest spots on the Fred Allen radio show. These were followed by similar appearances on the Bob Hope radio show, where he became a virtual fixture, needling Hope with bombastic insults and gags. That opened the door to making movies with Bob Hope in the Road Films series, he appeared in: *The Road to Singapore* (1940) as Achilles Bombassa, *The Road to Rio* (1947) as a cavalry captain, and *The Road to Hong Kong* (1962). He was credited with coining such catch phrases as "who's Yehudi?" and "ah, yes…exciting, isn't it?" It was evident that Bob Hope not only enjoyed working with Colonna but also formed a personal friendship with him.[9] Colonna continued to work in vaudeville and night-clubs until he suffered a partially-paralytic stroke in 1966 that curtailed his work opportunities. Fortunately Bob Hope did not forget him, as he found ways to work Jerry into his television specials without his disability becoming obvious.

Earlier, during his years playing in bands, he went on a blind date and met Florence Purcell, a pretty dancer who also came from Boston. They married in 1930 and adopted a baby son, Robert, in 1941. In 1979, Jerry suffered a heart attack that led to his confinement at the Motion Picture and Television Hospital, where he spent the final seven years of his life. Florence was at his side when Jerry died in 1986. She died eight years later.

Destined to become one of the funniest comedians of his era, Lou Costello (Louis Francis Cristillo) was born in Paterson, New Jersey in 1906, to an Italian father from Calabria, and a mother of French and Irish ancestry who Lou's daughter described as "a bastion of orthodox Catholicism."[10] Moviegoers, who first became familiar with a roly-poly, five-foot-five Costello in comedy roles, might be surprised to learn that he was a gifted high school athlete whose basketball proficiency propelled him to a New Jersey state foul-shot championship.[11] Although his accomplishments in baseball and boxing, fighting under the name of Lou King, earned him an athletic scholarship to Cornwall-on-Hudson Military School, he dropped out before graduation in order to try a performing career in Hollywood. He was yielding to a childhood dream to be in show business, one discernible beginning at age four and continuing throughout his youth as he playacted at home, clowned around in school, and sneaked into neighborhood movie houses. However, when the only work he could find in Hollywood was that of a stuntman who specialized in spectacular falls, (a background that would become useful in his later movie career, in which he performed his own stunts) he began to hitchhike back home, but only got as far as St. Joseph, Missouri, where he worked as a comedian in burlesque houses. In 1936, he found his ideal straight man in Bud Abbott, who also had a burlesque background, and together the team began to climb the entertainment ladder that would lead them to fantastic success by the early 1940s, in radio, Broadway, and motion pictures.

Abbott and Costello's first major screen hit, *Buck Privates* (1941), a zany comedy in which the two join the army to avoid jail, only to find out that their nemesis in civilian life is their drill instructor in boot camp, is considered by critics as not only the best Abbott and Costello movie, but also as one of the best comedy films of all time. It was the first service comedy based on the peacetime draft of 1940 and led to two more Abbott and Costello service comedies made before the nation entered war, *In The Navy* (1941) and *Keep 'Em Flying* (1941). In 1947, they made a sequel called *Buck Privates Come Home*. For the next decade, they reigned as Hollywood's biggest comedic team, indeed Lou became internationally known as he portrayed the persona of the exploited, luckless, unfortunate pawn of his conniving partner. Altogether the duo made thirty-six films between 1940 and 1956, and became among the most popular and highest-paid entertainers who performed on the radio as well as on the screen.

Lou teamed up with Abbott in their most famous routine, "Who's On First?," which has become a classic of American comedy. A reprise of an old skit that had been presented in vaudeville for years, it was a clever play on words in which Abbott queries Lou about the names of a mythical baseball team whose members have strange names: Who, who plays first base; What, who plays second base; I Don't Know, who plays third base; and so on, thereby totally confusing and exasperating Lou. Abbott and Costello first performed the routine on the popular radio program *The Kate Smith Hour* and reprised it, with modifications, in movies. The sketch was so amusing that President Roosevelt, who regarded it as his favorite comic sketch, personally requested they perform it for him; its recording is a popular feature in the Baseball Hall of Fame in Cooperstown, New York. In 1999, *Time* magazine named the routine as the best comedy sketch of the twentieth century.

In 1934, Lou Costello married burlesque dancer Anne Battler, a marriage that produced three children but one that also suffered a tragedy when their infant son, Lou Jr., not yet one year old, accidentally drowned in the family pool in 1942. Notified of the child's death, Lou, in keeping with show business tradition that "The show must go on," went on with his radio show. After problems with the Internal Revenue Service, which put a serious crimp in their financial situation, the famous Abbott and Costello duo split up in 1957, whereupon Costello pursued a solo standup career, including stints in Las Vegas, television shows and a film. In March 1959, at age fifty-two Costello died of a heart attack. A funeral Mass was said at his parish, St. Francis de Sales Catholic Church in Sherman Oaks, California, and he is interred at Calvary Cemetery, East Lost Angeles. Within the same year, his wife died. At the approach of the centenary of his birth in 2006, the city of Paterson renamed Madison Street, the street where he was born, Lou Costello's Place, and erected a life-sized bronze of the comedy genius titled *Lou's On First*, in which he is depicted carrying a bat and wearing his trademark derby.[12]

As an accomplished musician: a singer, an actor, a songwriter, and a trumpeter, Louis Prima may not immediately come to mind when discussing Italian American comedians. Known from the 1920s through the 1960s for, initially, his New Orleans jazz band, followed by a swing big band and pop-rock bands, he continually informed his material with humor, much of it evoking his Sicilian ancestry. His appeal also emanated from performances that evoked the unique African American environment in which he was raised. "I grew up in a hard-working, tough, mixed New Orleans block...My mother swapped food and friendship with the colored families, and I chased the parade bands and the funeral processions," he explained. Born and raised in New Orleans, Prima absorbed the prevailing milieu in the city that was the home of Jazz, the incomparable form of American music that produced such icons as Louis Armstrong. Born in 1910 to Anthony Prima (a soda-pop distributor) and Angelina Caravella, a strong-willed housewife who organized church activities and was also an amateur performer, music was a strong presence in his household. Like other Italian Americans in Little Palermo, the Prima family worshipped in St. Ann's Catholic Church, where Louis was baptized and partook of Italian religious customs, such as the festive celebration of St. Joseph's Day.[13] Like his brother and sister, Louis originally took violin lessons, but he turned to the trumpet as he swerved toward the entertainment field for a livelihood. Possessor of an exuberant personality, he attended Jesuit High School in New Orleans before being dismissed because of misbehavior. As discussed previously, songwriting was among his many talents. He composed swing songs, including "Jump, Jive an' Wail," and achieved extraordinary renown for "Sing, Sing, Sing," which merited him a major place in the field of swing music. The latter

> is generally viewed as one of the greatest jazz riffs, with a dramatic and extended drum solo, of all time, even though as the years went

by Goodman, rather than Prima, became more publicly linked and associated with the tune.[14]

While acknowledging his many talents, scholars conclude; "Prima is best known for his contributions as a performer who had the ability to make people laugh at his humorous lyrics and comedy routines." His live band performances illustrated an exuberance and vitality that also show-cased his Italian background, as evident in songs like "Angelina," with lyrics about pizza, veal parmegiana, pasta fagiole, and antipasto—exotic sounding words to Americans, although familiar within Italian American circles.[15] He followed this with similar, unmistakable, Italian American lyrics in "Josephina," "Please No Squeeza Da Banana," "Bacciagaloop, Makes Love on the Stoop," "Felicia No Capicia." In numerous instances his songs are sprinkled with words reflecting his Sicilian background—one example is his rendition of "Just A Gigolo (I A'int Got Nobody)" in which he sings the Sicilian word *nuddo* for "nobody" instead of the Italian *nessuno*. The repertoire of Prima's songs that reflect an Italian heritage, sometimes sung in both English and Italian, helped raise Italian American consciousness to new heights. A versatile performer, in 1967 he became the voice of King Louis, the orangutan in the Walt Disney animated movie production of *The Jungle Book,* which was nominated for an Oscar. Interestingly, although Prima was briefly part of the Hollywood scene, it was never a main springboard for him because, as a jazz musi-cian, the social importance of the music in which he specialized seemed beyond Hollywood's capability to understand. "Louis's films were only a means to showcase his talent. But even in this limited context, Prima was able to project, to come across to the audience primarily because he was such a superb performer."[16]

Louis Prima was married five times, had three children, and died of complications following a brain tumor on August 24, 1978, in New Orleans. Louis' music and compositions live on, however, and have appeared in numerous motion pictures, television programs, and adver-tisements. His memory lives on in New Orleans where, on the centenary of his birth, in 2010, he was the highlight of the fourteenth Annual New Orleans International Music Colloquium in the French Quarter Festival.

Comedienne Ruth Buzzi, who was born in Westerly, Rhode Island in 1936, was the daughter of Rena Pauline and Angelo Peter Buzzi, a nationally recognized stone sculptor, who created majestic marble eagles at New York's Penn Station, among other works. She attended Stonington High School, studied dancing, and enrolled at the Pasadena Playhouse, where she began to develop some of the comedic characters for which she would become famous. Although she played in a number of musical and comedy stage plays, including *Sweet Charity*, her most lasting impact was on television, as a member of a repertory company variety show and as a regular on sitcoms like *That Girl* and especially *Laugh-In*. Other memorable television stars with whom she has appeared were Dom DeLuise and Dean Martin. Ruth, frequently seen in *Sesame Street*, has provided voices for *Pound Puppies,* the *Berenstain Bears*, and Hanna-Barbera cartoons and also had roles in twenty films. Among her more substantial parts were Damsel In Distress in *The Villains* (1979), Marilyn, the femme fatale in *Up Your Alley* (1989), and Grandma Maw, in *Troublemakers* (1994). Ruth is married and lives in Texas.[17]

Josephina Victoria Occhiuto (Joy Behar), born in Brooklyn, New York in 1942, was the only child of Rose, a sewing machine operator, and Louis, a truck driver. She received a Bachelor of Arts degree from Queens College and a Master of Arts degree in Education from Stony Brook University and taught English for a few years at Lindenhurst High School. Her marriage to Joe Behar, which ended in divorce, produced a daughter named Eve. Unfulfilled as a teacher, she left to study acting and entered show business in the field of comedy, in time becoming a leading comic, who worked in television and movies intermixing interviews with incongruous juxtapositions. Her film credits include *Cookie* (1989), *Good Morning America* (1975), and *Love Is All There Is* (1996). She is better known for her television roles for and her acerbic criticism of public figures she dislikes and has received spirited criticism for being an opinionated and antireligious left-winger. Apparently reveling in the notoriety, Behar maintains that in projecting her views she reflects the environment in which was raised: the Italian American milieu of the post–World War II era undergoing fundamental change.

Floyd Vivino (Uncle Floyd) is a contemporary Italian American comedian whose long career, while mostly in television and radio, also included a dramatic role as Buddy Kirk, a New York disk jockey dealing with the tensions of the time, in the movie *Good Morning, Vietnam* (1987). Among his other film appearances are a bit part as Eddie Aris in the comedy *Crazy People* (1990), as M.C. in *Mr. Wonderful* (1993), and as AssPincher in *A Pyromaniac's Love Story* (1995). He was born in Paterson, New Jersey in 1951 into a show business family; his father played the trumpet, his mother was an actress and his two brothers play musical instruments in a band that performs for television shows. He studied dance and piano as a youngster but preferred to make people laugh. For twenty-four years he had a cable-television comedy show in the Philadelphia and New Jersey market that was a parody of children's shows and which featured slapstick, puppetry, and audience participation. Very knowledgeable about his Italian ancestry, Floyd has been known to "Italian Americanize classic songs such as his version of 'The Twelve Days of Christmas' in which Vivino substituted Italian food (ziti, meatballs, mozzarella, etc.)."[18] He also hosts *The Italian American Serenade* radio show, which features Italian music, boasting he has the largest collection of Italian records outside of Italy.

CHARACTER ACTORS

Along with principal actors, character actors' faces are familiar to veteran filmgoers, even if they do not always recognize their names or the names of their characters—indeed, character actors sometimes play generic parts without specific screen names. As one who is cast in a predominantly supporting part rather than a lead, a character actor can play roles ranging from bit parts to secondary leads. Notwithstanding the fact that the roles they play in films are seemingly minor, character actors nevertheless play important and sometimes indispensable roles vital to the credibility of a movie. Character-acting roles are determined partly by choice and partly by opportunity. The best character actors can bring distinction the smallest of roles. Like all professional actors, they subscribe to the principle that acting is an art, that the actor must have talent, instinct and control of a situation.[19] Character actors often play in roles that are not subject to a major change in the course of the plot. By utilizing his or her imagination and engaging in research to thoroughly familiarize him- or herself with a screen role, it is the job of the character actor to bring substance to the character. It has been said that the very best character actors are made of equal parts discipline and madness—discipline to depict their portrayals as believably as possible, and madness because their faces are more familiar than their names. Ubiquitous yet unfamiliar, character actors are not stars in the sense that fans stampede to movies because they are in them. "Character actors seldom appear throughout a film and are rarely granted long, adoring close-ups. Scripts aren't written for them. Agents don't fawn over them."[20] Employment is not steady and they may easily become typed in character roles: psychopath, drinking buddy, and the like. Male character actors seldom kiss the beautiful star. Thus, their goal in films in not to win the public's adulation, but rather to bring credibility to countless anonymous people who help round out our lives. In his study of the character actor, Mel Gussow, the noted theater critic of the *New York Times* pointed out that though the difference between principal roles and supporting roles can be arbitrary, they nevertheless it can be totally rewarding not only to the character actor but also to the audience.[21]

A review of Hollywood and Italian American actors confirms the validity of the above observation. Over the years, untold numbers of Italian Americans have been cast in movies in minor or subordinate roles, and while some have succeeded to the level of leading actors, thereby achieving worldwide stardom, many more have performed and continue to act in lesser but nonetheless satisfying parts as character actors. We have already examined the careers of some, like Frank Puglia, Henry Armetta, Eduardo Cianelli, Joseph Calleia, and Mimi Aguglia under different categories, and we now turn to other notable examples: Anthony Caruso, Michael Gazzo, Robert John Davi, Dennis Farina, Burt Young, Robert Loggia, Patty (Russo) McCormack, Diane Venora, Steve Buscemi, Paul Giamatti, and Claire Forlani.

Anthony Caruso, born to Italian immigrant parents in 1916 in Frankfurt, Indiana, moved with his family at age ten to Long Beach, California, where the family assisted relatives in running a restaurant. Given his famous last name, he originally thought of becoming a singer, but soon decided on a future in the acting profession instead and, like other budding actors, struggled to establish his acting career.[22] His chance meeting and befriending of another Long Beach Poly High student, Alan Ladd, whom he treated to lunch and who, like Anthony, sought a scholarship at the Pasadena Playhouse, was fortuitous. Years later, Ladd, who had become famous for his role in *This Gun for Hire* (1942), specifically requested that Caruso be cast in movies with him. It was the beginning of a collaboration that would see Caruso garner roles in eleven Alan Ladd films, including one of Caruso's best parts as the villainous gambler Jack Sturdevant in *The Iron Mistress* (1952). He became a regular stock player for Ladd's movie production company, an association highlighted by his role in the cult film *The Asphalt Jungle* (1950), in which he plays an Italian American professional safecracker who agrees to take part in an elaborately planned jewel robbery but is mortally wounded and taken home, where he dies surrounded by his large family.

Throughout his long career, Anthony Caruso was one of the cinema's notable villains. However, he was also one of the most versatile character actors, portraying Italians along with many other ethnic figures, including Native Americans, Greeks, Mexicans, Spaniards and Slavs. Thus he could be seen variously as a heroic American fighter in war films like *Pride of the Marines* (1945); in Bob Hope comedies including *Monsieur Beaucaire* (1946), *My Favourite Brunette* (1947) and *Where There's Life* (1947); as well as in Tarzan films such as *The Leopard Woman* (1946) and *Tarzan and the Slave Girl* (1950); and as the renegade, troublemaker Indian chief Natchakoa, in *Cattle Queen of Montana* (1954). Television provided another outlet for Caruso's acting talent, where he appeared in numerous western shows like *The Lone Ranger*, *Gunsmoke*, *Laramie* and *Wagon Train*.

Caruso's screen persona as a villain with gruff mannerisms and dark, rugged looks belied his real lifestyle. He was considered a model citizen in his beloved community of Brentwood, California, where he returned home every night after work to cook or tend his garden and where he served on various civic committees, attended church regularly, helped numerous charities and organizations, and worked closely with youngsters as a Boy Scout troop leader. Given his family's background in the restaurant business, Anthony, not surprisingly, enjoyed cooking authentic Italian dinners for cast members and crews on the sets of movies on which he happened to be working. He was devoted to his wife Tonia, with whom he stayed married for sixty-three years until the time of his death, in 2003, at age eighty-six. In addition to his wife, his daughter Tonia Valente, an actress, and a son Tonio are survivors.[23]

One of the most familiar character actors of the movies, as well as the stage and television, of the 1970s and 1980s was Vincent Gardenia, born in Naples, Italy in 1922 as Vincente Scognamiglio. Born into an Italian acting family that emigrated to Brooklyn, New York when he was two years old, he began his acting career as a child performing in a family acting troupe in Italian American neighborhoods in and around New York City.[24] He played minor roles until the late 1960s, by which time the man with a short, stocky build, exaggerated gestures, and a distinctive, booming voice had become widely acknowledged as a major acting talent. He excelled on the Broadway stage, winning a Tony Award for Best Featured Actor in a Play for his role in *Prisoner of Second Avenue* (1972), and was nominated for Best Actor in a Musical for his performance in *Ballroom* (1979). He also appeared in a number of films, reaching peaks that earned him Academy

Award nominations as Best Supporting Actor in *Bang The Drum Slowly* (1973) and *Moonstruck* (1987). Gardenia, who was the virtual embodiment of a character actor, was aptly described by a journalist who interviewed him in his home in Brooklyn as he tendered his tomato plants.

> He doesn't look like a matinee idol. That day he was wearing a faded green bandon shirt over his fat belly. His brown polyester pants were hitched up somewhere underneath his stomach and went flat in the rear. He wore no shoes and one stocking needed a few stitches in the heel.[25]

A versatile actor whose repertoire ranged from comedy to drama, he loved to act and estimated that he played some five hundred roles throughout his career. "I climbed on the stage when I was five years old and I've hardly stepped off since. If it were up to me I'd work fifty-two weeks a year." He died of a heart attack while on an acting assignment in Philadelphia in 1992 and is interred in St. Charles Cemetery in Farmingdale, Long Island. A section of 16th Avenue in Bensonhurst, Brooklyn, where he lived until his death, bears the secondary name of Vincent Gardenia Boulevard.[26]

The first significant theatrical success of Michael Vincent Gazzo was as a playwright. Born in Hillside, New Jersey, in 1923, he used the G.I. Bill scholarship he earned while serving in the Air Force during World War II to attend a Dramatic Workshop at the New School. The result was his writing *A Hatful of Rain*, a trenchant drama regarding drug abuse that enjoyed Broadway success as it ran for 389 performances and won Tony Acting nominations for two of its stars, Ben Gazzara and Anthony Franciosa. The play was made into a Hollywood movie in 1957 and was nominated for major awards.[27]

After the flop of his second Broadway play, Gazzo turned to screenwriting for a number of years, founded the Gazzo Theater Workshop in Los Angeles, and in 1974 finally became a character actor. Serious about his work, he was sensitive to ridicule and did not appreciate jokes at the expense of his efforts. He got his big break in *Godfather Part II* when he landed the part of Frankie Pentangeli, a role previously rejected by Richard Castellano ,but one in which Gazzo acted so well that it propelled him to an Oscar nomination for his portrayal—losing out on the award to his costar Robert De Niro. Possessing a stocky physique and piercing screeching voice, he continued his career as a first-rate character actor, frequently being typecast as Mafiosi and other criminal types. He was able to break away from the stereotype, however, in a number of his recurrent television appearances, in which he played more constructive parts. He died of a stroke in February, 1995 in his hometown of Hillside, New Jersey, at the age of seventy-one, leaving as survivors his wife, Grace, a daughter and two sons.

The Sicilian roots of actor Robert Loggia, whose birth name was Salvatore, are no more remote than his parents, Elena Blandino, a homemaker, and Benjamin Loggia, a shoemaker, both of whom were born in Sicily. Robert, who was born in Staten Island, New York in 1930, went to New Dorp High School, Wagner College, and then, as the recipient of a football scholarship, the University of Missouri before entering the Army, where he gained radio experience. Although his college major was journalism, he decided to enter the acting field after experiencing the exhilaration of performing on the stage in a college production of *The Taming of the Shrew*. He then studied at New York's Actors Studio, where he began to act in numerous stage productions and also had a small role in his first movie, *Somebody Up There Likes Me* (1956). He was soon cast in larger roles in films such as *The Garment Jungle* (1957), a shocking union drama in which he convincingly portrayed Tulio Renata, an organizer for the International Ladies Garment Union who is killed by goons, and in *The Greatest Story Ever Told* (1965), where he played Joseph, stepfather of Jesus. Throughout the course of his long career, he has played tough-talking cops and thugs, notably in *Scarface* (1983), *Prizzi's Honor* (1985), and *The Sopranos*. He appeared in short-lived television sequences, a few daytime soap operas, and played a notable lead role as Nick Mancuso in the television series *Mancuso, FBI*, which earned him a nomination for an Emmy Award. His numerous character-actor roles in films include parts in several *Pink Panther* films and an alcoholic father in *An Officer and a Gentleman* (1982). He also appeared in *Piedone d'Egitto* (1979), an Italian-language film.

Loggia is one of those selfconfident people who seemed to come to acting naturally. "I wasn't nervous at all. I was completely comfortable on stage," is the way he described his first college stage appearance. He reached a peak in his Hollywood acting career in the courtroom thriller *Jagged Edge* (1985), which starred Glenn Close and Jeff Bridges and for which Robert received an Oscar nomination as Best Supporting Actor for his portrayal of a coarse private investigator. Among the dozens of films in which Loggia has appeared are *Big* (1998), *Independence Day* (1996), and *Wide Awake* (1997). Loggia has been married twice; he had three children with his first wife, Marjorie Sloan, and one child and a stepdaughter with his second wife, Audrey O'Brien. He acknowledges his character-actor career in a thoughtful way: "I'm a character actor in that I play many different roles, and I'm virtually unrecognizable from one role to another, so I never wear out my welcome." He continues to perform effectively as an actor into his eighties.[28]

Burt Young, one of the most talented character actors of the last two generations, was born Gerald Tommaso DeLouise in Corona, Queens, New York in 1940. His pre-acting career was characterized by an assort-ment of activities, including serving in the Marines and working as a carpet installer and cleaner, a salesman, and an amateur boxer who fought dozens of times and who counts among his friends boxing stars George Foreman and Mohammed Ali. Seeking a career in acting, he studied dramatic arts at the Actors Studio and was fortunate to be a student of legendary acting coach Lee Strasberg—a valued background that led to appearances in motion pictures like *The Gang That Couldn't Shoot Straight* (1971), *Across 110th Street* (1972), and *Chinatown* (1974), in which he was usually cast as a harsh and tough Italian American char-acter, befitting his burly physical presence. More than any other, it was his role as the ill-mannered Paulie Pennino, future brother-in-law of Rocky (Sylvester Stallone) in *Rocky* (1976), which brought him to the public's attention. The role also earned him the distinction of an Academy Award nomination for Best Supporting Actor. He would reprise the role in all five of the *Rocky* sequels. Young, who has appeared in over one hundred films and television shows, is also a talented artist—he won a New York City-wide art contest when he was twelve years old—who owns and operates an art studio in Port Washington, New York, where he exhibits his art work. A widower who has performed on stage with his actress daughter, Anne Morea, he is, in addition, a writer who has penned two plays.[29]

Dennis Farina is another familiar contemporary character actor. Born in 1944 in Chicago, Illinois to Yolanda, a homemaker, and Joseph Farina, a Sicilian doctor, he was one of seven children. Although he liked going to movies when he was young, Dennis never took formal acting lessons and, in fact, became a policeman in Chicago, where he was already an eighteen-year veteran when he was hired to become a local consultant for the film *Thief* (1981) and got a bit part as a villain in the movie. He continued to do some acting while still on the police force, until 1986, when he left the force after director Michael Mann signed him up for a television series, *Crime Stories*. Mann also cast Farina as Detective Jack Crawford in the stylish thriller *Manhunter* (1986). Films like *Midnight Run* (1988) and *Get Shorty* (1995) demonstrate Farina's comedic flare. Indeed, he won the ASCAP Film and Television Music Award in 1995 as the Funniest Supporting Actor in a Motion Picture. As Farina's acting career progressed, his charm, self-effacement and audacity made an ineffaceable impression, described by one writer as "the kind of friendly guy you'd swear you once met at a bar, on a plane, in a hotel lounge or in a golf clubhouse. And if you hadn't, you'd had."[30]

Farina's versatility, ranging from playing a villain, gangster, detective, army officer, or a comedy role, found him playing in numerous films such as Saving Private Ryan (1998) and The Mod Squad (1999), while also being cast in starring roles in popular television shows like *Law and*

Order. The father of three sons and grandfather of one granddaughter and four grandsons, he is divorced from Patricia. In 2008, Farina had trouble with the law for carrying a loaded pistol through airport security; he had forgotten it was still in his briefcase. He entered a plea bargain and the charges were subsequently dismissed and expunged from Farina's otherwise clean record. Responding to a query about the fun in being a character actor as opposed to the lead, Dennis made a trenchant observation.

> In a sense, all actors are character actors, because we're all playing different characters. But a lot of the time—and I don't know, because I'm not a writer—but writers a lot of times write second- and third-tier characters better than they write primary characters. I guess they're more fun. I've sure had fun.[31]

Born in 1945 in Brooklyn, New York as Patricia Ellen Russo, Patty McCormack was the daughter of fireman Frank Russo and Elizabeth McCormack, a professional roller skater. Born with a lisp that required corrective work with a speech therapist, four-year-old Patty was entered, at the urging of an aunt, into a modeling contest that led to a contract and to a name change from Russo to McCormack. Although they did not force her, Patty's parents went along with the idea of a genuine child actress, a four-year-old model who began making television appearances at age seven and who shortly afterwards made her screen debut, an uncredited role in *Two Gals and a Guy* (1951). While she continued to appear in television shows like the *Mama* series, she also began to act on stage, making her Broadway debut in 1953. In 1952 Patty was cast as Rhoda Penmark, a veritable demon in child's garb, in the stage rendition of *Bad Seed,* for which she received much critical acclaim. Patty reprised the role in the 1956 Gothic horror thriller *Bad Seed,* where she shocked audiences with her performance as a seemingly innocent pert, blond girl with braided pigtails that hid a malicious and evil sociopathic personality. *Bad Seed* went on to be nominated for several Academy Awards, including a nomination for Patty McCormack as Best Supporting Actress. She also received a similar nomination for a Golden Globe. She continued to be cast in young roles for several years in unremarkable movies like *Jack-town* (1962), *The Mini-Skirt Mob* (1968) and *Maryjane* (1968).

In 1957, Patty married Bob Catania, a restaurateur, and had two children with him before the marriage was dissolved. For the next several years, she continued to act in supporting roles in a few movies and on television where, over the course of five decades, she has appeared in some two hundred fifty shows, mostly in secondary roles. In more recent years, she was cast in several movies, perhaps the most notable being *Frost/Nixon* (2008), in which she played Richard Nixon's wife, Pat, a casting that elicited the following observation:

> The creepiest, most jarring and perversely appropriate aspect of Frost/Nixon is the casting of Patty McCormack as Pat Nixon. She has precious few moments on the screen, but the fact that McCormack remains famous for her very-scary role in The Bad Seed only underlines the role that Pat played here—a ghostly, taut-faced, plainly painted reminder of how very wrong the Nixon presidency went.[32]

Vincent Schiavelli, selected in 1997 by *Vanity Fair* magazine as one of the best character actors in America, and born in 1948 to a Sicilian American family in Brooklyn, New York, was educated at Bishop Loughlin Memorial High School and New York University, where he studied theater. Standing six foot six, he looked down at his surroundings with droopy eyes and, because of his affliction with Marfan's Syndrome, projected a gloomy and dour physical appearance. Meeting this unusual countenance for the first time could be offputting, however, Schiavelli was a talented individual who acted on the stage and in television. He was also an acknowledged gourmand who wrote respected and award-winning cook books and articles on cooking, in addition to appearing in some 120 movies, where, as befitting his looks, he frequently played creepy or eccentric characters.[33]

He made his first film, *Taking Off,* in 1971 and had roles in dozens of movies, including some memorable turns, such as a mental ward patient in *One Flew Over the Cuckoo's Nest* (1975), Salieri's valet in *Amadeus* (1984), and a belligerent ghost in the film *Ghost* (1990). Schiavelli, who was married twice and was the father of two children, died at age fifty-seven, in Sicily in 2005.

Diane Venora is a supporting actress who has also found billing in lead roles. She was born in 1952, the daughter of Marie and Robert Venora, who owned a drycleaning establishment in East Hartford, Connecticut. Diane attended local schools, including East Hartford High School, where she acted in musicals and serious plays. Though she initially thought she would like to become a beautician like her sister, her father insisted that she go to college. However, since she did poorly in math and science, she increasingly looked to the theater as a legitimate field of study in which those difficult subjects were not part of the curriculum. Ultimately, she won a scholarship to the Julliard School of Music. Upon graduation, she performed as a stage actress, highlighted by her performance in *Hamlet* at the New York Shakespeare Festival.

Diane's film debut was as a criminal psychologist in the 1981 horror film *Wolfen*, cited as an "engrossing, frightening and intelligent," movie by critic Vincent Canby. She won praise for her role as Chan Parker, the wife of jazz saxophonist Charlie Parker, in *Bird* (1988), in a performance that earned her the Golden Globe Award nomination for Best Supporting Actress and a New York Film Critic's award. Her role as Al Pacino's wife in *Heat* (1995) also generated high praise and she performed effectively in supporting roles in *The Jackal* (1997), *The 13th Warrior* (1999), and *The Insider* (1999). In a movie revolving around Italian American life, Diane appeared in *Looking for an Echo* (1999), a nostalgic story about a dispirited, Italian, middle-aged man named Vince (Armand Assante), formerly part of a popular musical group, whose wife has passed away, and who suddenly finds joy again when he falls in love with his nurse, played by Diane Venora.[34] Diane has played a range of roles that have elicited comments about her ability to play brassy women as well as women of delicate emotional nuances.[35] She has also been cast in the *Thunder Alley*

and *Chicago Hope* television series. Although Diane's marriage to cine-
matographer Andrzej Bartkowiak, in 1980, produced a daughter, Madzia,
it ended in divorce a number of years later. As a single mother, Diane took
a seven-year hiatus from acting, during which she raised her daughter,
taught disadvantaged children and acted in an occasional play. When her
daughter became older, Diane resumed her acting career in movies like
Stiletto (2008) and *All Good Things* (2010).

Robert John Davi is an example of a contemporary Italian American
who is an accomplished character actor. Born in Astoria, Queens, New
York in 1953, he is the son of Italian American parents: his mother is
of Italian ancestry while his father was born in southern Italy. Since
the extended Davi family, which moved to Long Island while he was a
youngster, included his grandparents, whose first language was Italian,
he learned the language as a child, as did his six siblings. He attended
Catholic primary and secondary schools (the latter was Seton Hall High
School), where he began to appear in plays such as *Macbeth* and then
went to Hofstra University, having been drawn there because of its Shakespearean theater. The ubiquitous classical music that filled the Davi house
undoubtedly led Robert to an interest in opera—indeed he has a clas-
sically-trained baritone voice—however, acting was his lifelong ambi-
tion. As he explained; "I have always liked cinema, and let's face it,
opera singers are just bad actors! I didn't want to translate myself in that
direction. My heroes were people like Spencer Tracy, Bogart, Mitchum,
Marvin, Richardson, Caine, all those sort." Determined to learn to act, he
went to New York City, where he worked as a waiter, sold produce at a
fruit-and-vegetable stand, and lived in a cheap railroad flat while taking
classes at Juilliard Acting School. Davi had the good fortune to study with
the legendary actress Stella Adler and also was a member of the Actors
Studio, where he studied under the tutelage of Lee Strassberg. He launched
his film career in 1977, when he auditioned for and gained a part in a Frank
Sinatra telefilm, *Contract on Cherry Street* (1978). Davi, who idolized
Sinatra, even emulating his singing style, could not have been happier.
"Growing up in an Italian household, you have two figures, Sinatra and

the Pope. Sinatra had a huge singing career and a huge film career, so as a young Italian Sicilian kid, I looked to that career and had my sights on that, too. I had a commonality with Sinatra, who was the first singer to bring bel canto to popular music."[36]

From that point on, Davi, the rugged, six-foot-tall, 185-pound, broad-shouldered actor with a rugged and heavily pockmarked face, has become a fixture as a character actor, cast as a villain in many movies including the notorious Freddy Sanchez in *License to Kill* (1989), a James Bond thriller. He has played a gangster who likes to sing opera in *The Goonies* (1985) and has appeared in dozens of other films—indeed, his flexography lists over one hundred movies. He has also been cast as the Good Guy in the television series *Profiler* where, after meticulously researching the profiling profession, he starred as FBI Agent Bailey Malone for four and one half years, and earned critical acclaim for his authentic portrayal.[37] In 2007, Davi tried his hand at screenwriting and directing in a movie called *Dukes*, a comedy drama set in the 1960s that explored the impact a changing economic system wrought on blue-collar workers laid off from the work that they had been doing all their lives, men who were now trying to cope with the shock of being odd men out. Making the film was personally meaningful to Davi who, as a youngster, had witnessed the struggles of people dealing with the hard knocks of life and those who fell through the cracks, like his own father, a Navy veteran who suffered the indignity of being laid off. Also influenced by Italian Neo-realistic cinema, he meant for his movie to make a point about people caught up in stressful situation not of their own making and their attempts to deal with it in the wrong way—the paradox and the juxtaposition of honest people aware of their mortality and spiritual life, yet resorting to criminal ways in their desperation. A low-budget film that was not widely shown, *Dukes* nevertheless won critical praise at the Monte-Carlo Film Festival of Comedy, including Jury Prize for Best Screenplay, and Davi's work on the film won Queens Spirit Awards for Best Producer and Best Director.

Regarding himself as a devout Catholic, Davi has been a prominent Hollywood pro-life voice, yet he has been married three times and is the father of five children, four of them with his third wife, fashion model Christine Bolster. He is also one of a group of actors whose politics are decidedly conservative. He refers to the Bible in speaking out, lends support to a number of charitable functions of Italian American organizations such as the National Italian American Foundation and Unico, and is an advocate of animal rights, maintaining "It's no coincidence that the Bible describes God's instructions to Noah to take two of each animal. The story illustrates the love God has for all of his creatures. Our pets are family, too."[38] Davi continues to perform in various entertainment venues, including a return to singing in his 2010 *A Tribute to a Legend: Davi Sings Sinatra*.

Steve Buscemi, born in 1957 in East New York, Brooklyn, to Dorothy, an Irish American mother who worked as a restaurant hostess, and John Buscemi, a sanitation worker of Sicilian descent, had three brothers and was raised a Roman Catholic. When the family moved to Valley Stream, Long Island, Steve attended local schools, including Valley Stream Central High School, where he was a wrestling team member and where he became involved in the school's drama group. He attended Nassau Community College and the Lee Strassberg Institute while also working as a member of the New York City Fire Department in the Little Italy section of the city. His lasting ties to the Fire Department were evident on September 11, 2011, when the World Trade Center was destroyed, as he promptly returned to his old firehouse and spent many hours digging through rubble with his old comrades looking for missing firefighters. The enduring fraternal feeling among firefighters is remarkable. Most will admit to initial fear when entering a burning building, but it soon goes away and they operate on adrenaline. Going on the stage to perform can be likened to that experience. When he became a professional actor he made incisive an analogy linking acting with his fireman background.

He received praise for his first role in a major motion picture, *Parting Glances* (1987), that led to parts in many films, where he worked with some of the cinema world's most outstanding directors. He was often cast as a criminal in movies, that is, as a henchman in *King of New York* (1990), a homosexual bookie in *Millers Crossing* (1990), and an impulsive, loquacious, and murderous small-time felon/kidnapper in *Fargo* (1996). The frequency of these roles bemused him.

> It's weird; I was not a really tough guy in high school, but I end up playing all of these psychopaths and criminals. I don't really care who they are, as long as they are complicated and going through something that I can understand and put across.[39]

He came to the attention of a wider movie audience as a result of his role as a scratchy-voiced thief in *Reservoir Dogs* (1992), and continued to play to type in 2006 in the HBO series *The Sopranos,* in which his character is killed off. That role impressed one reviewer, who referred to Buscemi as "a distinguished character actor and certainly a distinctive one: bug-eyed and cadaverous, he speaks in a tinny voice that sounds like a 33 1/3 r.p.m. record played at 45." Buscemi continues to be typecast as a criminal in *Boardwalk Empire*, a 2010 HBO dramatic series directed by Martin Scorsese, albeit as an atypical, gaunt, reedy-voiced character who blends shrewdness with self-loathing.[40]

Talented and knowledgeable about acting, Buscemi is also interested in screenwriting and directing, achieving critical success with his first effort, *Trees Lounge* (1996), a comedy drama in which he also acted, playing the part of Tom Basilio, a forlorn Long Island auto mechanic who spends his days as a barfly interacting with the usual aimless working-class bar patrons. He readily acknowledges the film's autobiographical elements: "I was living a block away from the gas station where I worked and hanging out at a bar across the street from the gas station." When his friends went off to college, he remained behind to drive an icecream truck. "If I had stayed there, maybe I'd have just… " he says, trailing off into a shrug. "But I got out." He has also directed *Animal Factory* (2000) a film about surviving prison life, as well as episodes of HBO's *Oz* and *The Sopranos*. A working actor who lives in Park Slope, Brooklyn with his wife Jo Andres, a writer and filmmaker, and teenage son Lucian, a musician, Buscemi can sometimes be seen taking the F subway line.[41]

Paul Edward Valentine Giamatti, born in New Haven, Connecticut in 1967, has Italian ancestry through his father—A. Bartlett Giamatti who became nationally famous as Yale University's president and Commissioner of Major League Baseball—while his mother was of Irish descent. Paul began his theatrical career as an undergraduate student at Yale University and developed it further while earning a master's degree in fine arts at the Yale School of Drama, where he acted in numerous plays and on television. He made his mark as a character actor, for which he won critical acclaim in *Private Parts* (1997), *The Truman Show* (1998), *Saving Private Ryan* (1998) and *American Splendor* (2003). His role as the manager of fighter Jim Braddock in *Cinderella Man* (2005) won him a nomination for the Academy Award for Best Supporting Actor. Paul is married and has one son.

Born in 1972 in Twickerham, London, the daughter of a British mother and Italian music manager Pierluigi Forlani, Claire Forlani studied acting and dancing at the famed London Art Education School as a child and soon began to appear professionally in British television. Convinced that California offered greater acting opportunities, the Forlanis moved to California where, by 1993, she became a cast member in the *J.F.K.: Reckless Youth* television mini-series and the 1994 film *Police Academy: Mission to Moscow*. She was rewarded with larger roles in *Mallrats* (1994) a story about two young college students who respond to being jilted by their girlfriends by spending their time in a shopping mall, and *The Rock* (1996) in which she is cast as the estranged daughter of Sean Connery.

> In succeeding years Claire has appeared in a number of widely released and financially successful movies such as *Meet Joe Black* as well as smaller independent films. She also has had recurring roles in the popular television series "CSI". In addition to acting

she is considered one of the world's most beautiful women, and accordingly has been showcased in many glamour magazines. In 2007 Claire Forlani married Scottish actor Dougray Scott in a private civil ceremony in the Forlani family country home in Pieve-bovigliana Italy, where her father Pierluigi played a major role in planning and preparing the food and festivities for the reception.[42]

Corbin Blue, Demi Lovato, Chad Allen Lazzari, Lola Glaudini, Tony Sirico, Joe Vitarelli and Al Ruscio are among other Italian Americans who have established themselves as competent character actors and who, in some instances, have achieved meaningful lead parts.

ENDNOTES

1. John F. Mariani, "Everybody Likes Italian Food," American Heritage, Vol. 40, Issue 8, December 1989, 143.
2. John F. Mariani and Lidia Bastianich, *How Italian Food Conquered the World* (New York: Palgrave Macmillan, 2011). See also Jane Ferry, *Food in Film, A Culinary Performance of Communication* (New York: Routledge, 2003).
3. Dom DeLuise, *Eat This...It'll Make You Feel Better!* (New York: Pocket Books, 1990). This work has a great deal of material on growing up Italian in Brooklyn.
4. Interview with Ann DeLuise Dauria, November 2010.
5. Joseph Tropiano, introduction to *Big Night: a Novel With Recipes* (New York: St. Martin's Griffin, 1996).
6. *New York Post*, May 7, 2009.
7. For Durante's childhood see, Gene Fowler, *Schnozzola:The Story of Jimmy Durante* (New York: Viking, 1951), 3–15.
8. Bakish, Jimmy Durante.
9. See: Lawrence J. Quirk, *Bob Hope: The Road Well Traveled* (New York: Applause, 2000), 99; and William Robert Faith, *Bob Hope: A life in Comedy* (Cambridge, Massachusetts: Da Capo Press, 2003), 96,104–107, 133, 284.
10. Chris Costello, *Lou's on First, The Tragic Life of Hollywood's Greatest Clown* (New York: St. Martin's Griffin, 1982), 2.
11. Costello, *Lou's on First,* 5.
12. For a fascinating psychological analysis of Costello as the classic clown of "vaudevillian horror" films see John S. Bak, "Abbott and Costello meet ... John Hawkes: The Goose on the Grave, affect, and Tomkins's script theory," *Journal of Evolutionary Psychology* 29 (October. 2006):1–2.
13. Thomas Clavin, *That Old Black Magic: Louis Prima, Keely Smith and the golden age of Las Vegas* (Chicago: Chicago Review Press, 2010), 12–14; a good source of information regarding the early years of Italian-African American interaction.
14. Garry Boulard, *Louis Prima: Music in American Life* (Urbana: University of Illinois Press, 2002), 78.
15. Boulard, *Louis Prima,* 72; Clavin, *That Old Black Magic,* 11. Mere coincidence does not explain his recording of a Frank Kelton song named

Angelina—he was attracted to it because it was his mother's name—the person who had the most profound influence on his life.

16. Boulard, *Louis Prima*, 50. It is also of interest to learn that Guy Lombardo, associated with sweet music, encouraged Prima to come to New York City.

17. Kristie Ramirez, "Ruth Buzzi's Garage," *Texas Monthly*, Dec. 2010, 46.

18. See Primeggia, "Comedy," 130–137.

19. Sanford Meisner, *Sanford Meisner On Acting* (New York: Vintage Books, 1987), 25–31. See also Stella Adler *The Art of Acting* (New York: Applause Books, 2000), chap. 1.

20. Jill Geretson, "If They Look Familiar, It's Because They Are," *New York Times,* Oct 27, 1996.

21. Mel Gussow, "Character Actors Are Taking a Star Turn," *New York Times*, May 18, 1990.

22. See Lee Server, *Robert Mitchum: Baby, I Don't Care* (New York: St. Martin's Griffin, 2002), p. 45; for a description of how he and his beach buddy Robert Mitchum sought acting opportunities through the Federal Theater Company.

23. *The Independent*, April 8, 2003.

24. Emelise Aleandri, *The Italian American Immigrant Theater in New York City* (Charleston, South Carolina: Arcadia, 1999), 8. See also Emelise Aleandri, *Little Italy* (Charleston, South Carolina: Arcadia, 2002), 103

25. Joyce Curci, "Vincent Gardenia and His Tomato Plants," *The Italian American Review* 2, no. 1 (April 17, 1993): 137–139.

26. *Los Angeles Times*, December 10, 1992.

27. Michael Bacarella, *Italactors: 101 Years of Italian Americans in U. S. Entertainment* (Washington, D.C.: National Italian American Foundation, 1990).

28. *New York Times*, May 5, 2011.

29. Farah Weinstein, "'Rocky' Actor Burt Young: A Lover And A Fighter," *Port Washington Patch*, October 4, 2010.

30. Joel Drucker, "A Sweet Second Act," *Cigar Aficionado*, August 1, 1999.

31. Noel Murray, "Random Roles: Dennis Farina," *The A.V. Club*, Onion Inc., March 17, 2009, http://www.avclub.com/articles/dennis-farina,25185/.

32. Cynthia Fuchs, "FrostNixon," *Celebrity Wonder*, accessed May 10, 2012, http://celebritywonder.ugo.com/movie/2008_FrostNixon_cynthia_fuchs.html.

33. See, for example, Vincent Schiavelli, *Bruculinu, America* (New York, Houghton Miflin, 1998).

34. Dennis Harvey, "Looking For an Echo," *Variety*, October 25, 1999.

35. Marilyn Moss, "C.S. Lewis, Beyond Narnia," *Hollywood Reporter*, December. 9, 2005.
36. *Las Vegas Sun*, February 9, 2012
37. Paul Chutkow, "Playing the Heavy," *Cigar Aficionado,* December 1, 1996.
38. Washington Times, April 21, 2009.
39. David Carr, *New York Post*, March 23, 2006
40. Charles McGrath, *New York Times*, September 2, 2010
41. John Lahr, "The Thin Man," *The New Yorker*, November 14, 2005, 72.
42. Michelle Tan, *People*, June 08, 2007.

CHAPTER 8

ACADEMY AWARD WINNERS

Just as in other fields of endeavor that celebrate the highest levels of achievement within their crafts, individuals whose careers revolve around the motion picture industry honor their exceptional peers. In their case it is with glittering annual awards ceremonies that attract world-wide audiences—one billion people were said to have watched the Academy Awards ceremony in 2011. Because cinema is a popular, visual sphere filled with superstar celebrities, ceremonies that award honorees in cinema have resonance not only to movie industry personnel but also to a much wider public. There are, in fact, a number of prestigious venues that regularly and annually judge and designate awards for films, actors, actresses, directors, and others, including the National Society of Film Critics, the New York Film Critics Circle, the Los Angeles Film Festival, the Boston Society of Film Critics, the Houston Film Festival, the Golden Globes, the MTV Movie Awards, and the Cannes Film Festival, among others. One study finds that in any given year, 3,182 awards are given in the field of entertainment, with the Oscars standing at the pinnacle of prestige. "The Oscars will always be the Kentucky Derby—nay, the Super Bowl of showbiz kudos because they're prizes bestowed by the winners' peers."[1] Thus, while all the many awards confer distinction upon distin-

guished movies and gifted individual awardees, the Academy Awards of
the motion picture industry, popularly known as Oscars, are the most fashionable and influential of such honors. They are the category that will be
explored in this chapter, noting not only the films including Italian and
Italian American themes, actors, actresses, directors, producers, and the
like which have won Oscars, but also those which have experienced the
rare distinction of being nominated for these notable honors. This exami-
nation of persons of Italian background in the moviemaking industry will
thereby serve to effectively buttress the impression of greater input by
and recognition of Italian Americans in Hollywood, documenting their
expanding involvement, a theme commented upon by others, including
Pellegrino D'Acierno, who observed that whereas before the 1970s, especially before *The Godfather* trilogy, relatively few films dealt with Italian
American life, afterwards, the situation changed dramatically; a phenomenon reflected in the swelling number of major Oscar awards tendered to
Italian Americans. He provides a figure that fifteen percent of such awards
were given to Italian Americans in the 1927 to 1995 period.[2]

The birth of the Academy Awards, which are tendered by the Academy
of Motion Picture Arts and Sciences, can be traced to 1927, when the
industry's foremost producers, directors and actors, such as Louis B.
Mayer, Cecil B. DeMille, Irving Thalberg, Jesse Lasky, and Douglas Fairbanks, agreed to the concept of awarding honors to those chosen by
consensus among a special committee of their peers to have excelled in
their craft during the previous year. Although Italian American representation in that initial period was numerically small, it is significant to
note that Frank Capra functioned as one of the first presidents of the
Academy Awards (1935–1939), the only person of his ethnicity ever to
have served in that post, and that two Italian Americans were among the
early awardees: Frank Borzage (born Borzaga) and Frank Capra. Borzage
won the Best Director award twice, first for *Seventh Heaven* (1927),
becoming the first person ever to win the award for directing, and then
for *Bad Girl* (1931), while Capra was a three-time Best Director winner
with *It Happened One Night* (1934), which won a total of five Oscars;

Mr. Deeds Goes to Town (1936); and *You Can't Take it With You* (1938). In addition to his Oscar triumphs, the following films directed by Capra were Best Picture nominees: *Lady For a Day*, (1932–1933), *Lost Horizon* (1937), and *Mr. Smith Goes to Washington* (1939). He was also nominated in the Best Director category for his documentary *Prelude to War* (1943), part of the *Why We Fight* propaganda film series commissioned by the Office of War Information, and *It's a Wonderful Life* (1946). *It's a Wonderful Life,* Capra's favorite film, is a heartwarming and inspirational movie about a man in despair coming to the realization that his life is important not only to him, but to many others. Although this movie has become a classic Christmastime favorite, and was nominated for Best Picture, Best Actor, Best Director, Best Sound Recording, and Best Film Editing, it failed to actually capture a single Oscar statuette. Capra's last film, *Pocketful of Miracles* (1961) , which he both produced and directed, was nominated for three Academy Awards, though it failed to win any.

Another film director of Italian descent in the early era was talented Gregory La Cava (1892–1952), born in Towanda, Pennsylvania, the son of Pascal Nicholas, a linguist and musician, and Eva Wolz. La Cava, who studied at the Art Studio of Chicago and began his film work as an animator producing comic strips for William Randoph Hearst's newspapers, entered the Hollywood scene when the Hearst operation went into the moviemaking business.[3] He became a successful film director whose major successes included *My Man Godfrey* (1936), and *Stage Door* (1937). La Cava served as producer, director, and writer for *My Man Godfrey,* which was the first movie to be nominated in all four acting categories (Best Actor, Best Actress, Best Supporting Actor, and Best Supporting Actress); it received six nominations in all, including Best Director and Best Screenplay. Although it failed to win an Oscar, the film was deemed "culturally significant" by the United States Library of Congress and selected for preservation in the National Film Registry as one of the funniest movies of all time. *Stage Door* received four nominations including Best Director, but also failed to win an Oscar.

These humble but important beginnings that hearkened to the silent screen era formed the foundation for large numbers of Italian and Italian American moviemakers to build on and so leave an impressive legacy of their own. It has been asserted that movies centering around Italian and Italian American themes finally became victorious during the 1970s in the Best Picture Awards category; the winners included two *Godfather* films, (1972 and 1974) and *Rocky* (1976). It was also during the decade of the 1970s that Italian American directors like Francis Ford Coppola and Michael Cimino received Best Director Awards; they would soon be followed by several others, including Martin Scorsese.[4]

Be that as it may, the 1950s has a stronger claim for Italian American screen ascendancy—it was the watershed for Italians and Italian Americans in the film industry in so far as it was during that period that Hollywood began to tender awards in the Best Foreign Language Film category that honored Italian-made films: *La Strada* (1956) with Federico Fellini, director, and Dino De Laurentis, as coproducer, and *The Nights of Cabiria* (1957) with the same collaborators). By the mid-twentieth century, furthermore, it was no longer unusual for members of the ethnic group to be awarded honors for their work in the film industry. When Frank Sinatra won the Academy Award as Best Supporting Actor for his part as tough and undisciplined Italian American soldier Angelo Maggio in *From Here To Eternity,* in 1953, he had achieved a historic niche— he became the first person of his ethnic background to win the esteemed Best Supporting Actor honor. Significantly, whereas no actor of Italian ancestry had received the Best Actor Award in the first half of the twentieth century, the omission was rectified in 1955, when Ernest Borgnine became the first Italian American to win the coveted award for his role as a modest and unpretentious butcher in *Marty*—a feat that was achieved by eight others of Italian ancestry up to 2008. It was coincidentally during the same year, 1955, that Italian and Italian American actresses emerged to win Best Actress Award, commencing with Anna Magnani in her first English-language role as the widowed Italian American seamstress in *The Rose Tattoo*, an accomplishment achieved by four others up to 2008.

In winning her Best Supporting Actress Award in 1992 for her acting in *My Cousin Vinny*, Marisa Tomei became the first Italian American to be so honored. In 1958, Italian American Lester Anthony "Vincente" Minnelli scored a major triumph as director of *Gigi*, an elegant musical about a young courtesan set in turn-of-the-century Paris that received a record-breaking nine Academy Award, plus a special honorary award for Maurice Chevalier. Not to be forgotten is the fact that, although better known for musicals, Minnelli had nevertheless directed *The Bad and The Beautiful* (1952), a scathing portrait of Hollywood's manipulative, tawdry and callous mores that holds the record for most Oscars won—five: Best Actress in Supporting Role, Best Art Direction, Best Cinematography, Best Costume Design, and Best Screenplay—by a movie that was not nominated for Best Picture. In addition, the 1950s saw the showering of several more Academy Award nominations on Italians and Italian Americans: Best Actor to Frank Sinatra for *Man With the Golden Arm* (1955), Best Supporting Actor to, Sal Mineo in *Rebel Without Cause* (1955) , and Best Supporting Actress to Marisa Pavan in *The Rose Tattoo* (1955).

Altogether, eleven films directed by people of Italian descent have received the Best Picture Academy Award, while twenty-six nominations for the same award have gone to them as well. Only slightly less prestigious than actually winning the Academy Awards, nominations for the coveted Oscars are important as a measure of how highly peers value the work of those deemed worthy of consideration for the high honor; these designations, furthermore, serve as springboards for the attainment of more desirable film parts for the designees. Since 1953, nine Italian Americans have won Best Actor awards outright, five have won Best Actress awards, three have won Best Supporting Actor awards and three have won Best Supporting Actress awards.

Other than the movies that actually received the Best Picture Oscars, an impressive eighteen films either directed and/or produced by Italian Americans or marked by an Italian American theme have been nominated for the Best Picture Award. An astounding twenty-seven nominations for

Best Actor Awards have gone to Italian Americans, in addition to those who were nominated and won. Other than those which resulted in a win in this category, fourteen nominations have gone to Italian Americans for Best Actress Awards. Italian Americans have garnered nominations for twenty-five Best Supporting Actor awards, while ten have been nominated for Best Supporting Actress. It is in the category of Best Director nominations that Italian and Italian Americans have made truly stunning inroads, with thirty-one films under their direction receiving the honor, in addition to those that actually won.

There are a number of fascinating highlights that revolve around Italian-born Academy Award winners and nominees, among which are the singular achievements of actors and actresses like Anna Magnani who, although appearing in only four American films, won the 1955 Best Actress Award for her portrayal of Serafina Delle Rose, a widowed Sicilian immigrant in *The Rose Tattoo*—making her the first of her nationality to win in this Oscar category. Magnani, incidentally, was also nominated for her part as the Italian mail-order bride Gloria in *Wild is the Wind* (1957). This extraordinary Hollywood feat was duplicated by Sophia Loren, who won the Best Actress Oscar for her performance as an Italian mother trying to protect her young daughter amidst the dark days of war torn Italy in *Two Women* (1960). Loren, who was also nominated for Best Actress for her role in *Marriage Italian Style* (1964), remains the *only* actress to win an Oscar for work in a foreign-language film. In 1990, The Academy of the Motion Pictures Association presented Sophia Loren with an Honorary Academy Award, a statuette in recognition for her memorable cinematic performances. Often a Loren costar, Italian actor Marcello Mastroianni received more Oscar nominations for his foreign language roles—three—than any other actor. His nominations were for his work in *Divorce Italian Style* (1962) *A Special Day* (1977), and *Dark Eyes* (1987). Italian born Roberto Benigni was the first actor in fifty years to receive a nomination for Best Director and for Best Picture while simultaneously winning the Best Actor Oscar Award for his role as the sympathetic Holocaust victim in the film *Life is Beautiful* (1998). Lawrence Olivier last accomplished this feat in 1948 with his *Hamlet*.

Vittorio De Sica, one of Italy's greatest movie directors, whose *The Bicycle Thief* (1948) is acknowledged as one of the finest of all the films in the Neo-realism genre and one of the ten greatest movies of all time, did not receive an Academy Award for the production because its release in 1949 predated the establishment of an official category for Best Foreign Language Film, which became a reality in 1956. The Academy Awards Institute sought to correct this oversight by honoring De Sica with a special Academy Award. De Sica's contemporary, Federico Fellini, was still another Italian-born filmmaker who made a considerable impact in Hollywood. Born in 1920, he received his first Academy Award nomination for Best Screenplay for the film *Open City* (1945), directed and produced by Roberto Rossellini; a second nomination for Best Screenplay for *Paisa* (1946), a film which also earned a nomination for Best Director for Roberto Rossellini; another nomination for Best Screenplay for *La Dolce Vita* (1960), which won an Oscar for Best Costumes in Black and White; and Oscar nominations for Best Director and Best Screenplay (with Tullio Pinelli) for *Il Vitelloni* (1953). Fellini won an Oscar for producing the Best Foreign Film and for Best Screenplay for *La Strada* (1954), which featured his wife Giulietta Masimo as Gelsomina, and won the Best Foreign Film for *Nights of Cabiria* (1957) which starred his wife, the Best Foreign Language Film Oscar for *81/2*, (1963) which also won an Oscar for Best Costumes and earned Fellini a nomination for Best Director. He was also nominated for Best Director for *Satyricon* (1969), and his 1974 movie *Amarcord* won the Oscar for Best Foreign Language Film and was also nominated for the Oscars for Best Director and Best Writing, Original Screenplay for this movie. His 1976 film *Fellini's Casanova* won an Oscar for Best Costumes. In April 1993, Fellini received his fifth Oscar, for lifetime achievement. While receiving a standing ovation he begged the audience to sit down and wittily remarked; "I should be the only one who is uncomfortable."[5]

Italian director Michelangelo Antonioni, who was acclaimed one of Italy's greatest twentieth-century directors and was the recipient of numerous awards, was liberally praised by movie critics for writing the screenplay for, and directing, the movie *Blow Up* (1966). Antonioni received Academy Award nominations for both Best Screenplay and Best Director and although he was denied both, the Academy Awards did present him with a special honorary award in 1994. Lina Wertmuller's movie *Seven Beauties* (1975), which she both wrote and directed, was nominated for Academy Awards for Best Actor in a Leading Role, Best Director, Best Foreign Language Film and Best Original Screenplay. Wertmuller was the first woman ever nominated for an Academy Award for Best Director. Dino De Laurentiis, another Italian cinema giant, born in 1919 near Naples, who would later move to the United States, became one of the leading producers of Neo-realistic films in postwar Italy. A prolific moviemaker, he was credited with producing more than five hundred films, including such classics as *Riso Amaro* (*Bitter Rice,* 1949), which was nominated for the Academy Award for Best Story in 1950. Once the husband of actress Silvana Mangano, De Laurentiis won an Oscar in 1956 for *La Strada* and altogether received Oscars thirty-eight times. In 2001, the Academy Awards Institute honored him with the Irving G. Thalberg Memorial Award for the high quality of his productions.

Among the unusual points about Academy Award–winning Italian American actors is the unique fact that a father, mother, and daughter in one family were recipients of the cherished honor: Liza Minnelli won a Best Actress Oscar for *Cabaret* (1970); her mother, Judy Garland, won a Special Juvenile Award in 1940; while her father, Vincente, won his award as the director of *Gigi* (1958). During the course of Vincente's career he directed seven different actors in Oscar-nominated performances.

Angelica Huston, the daughter of Enrika (Ricki) Soma, of Italian descent, won the Academy Award for Best Supporting Actress in *Prizzi's Honor* (1985), thereby becoming the third of her family so honored —her father, director John Huston, and grandfather, director and actor

Walter Huston, were also winners of Academy Awards. In 1989, Angelica received an Academy Award nomination for Best Supporting Actress for her work in *Enemies, a Love Story*, and in 1990 she was nominated for Best Actress for her acting in *The Grifters*.

Another award item of interest concerns Frank Sinatra who, before winning his Academy Award for Best Supporting Actor in *From Here to Eternity,* in 1953, had already won a special Honorary Oscar for his role in the short (ten minutes) documentary *The House I Live In* (1945). Produced in the last year of the Second World War, this documentary finds the young singer playing himself while intermingling with teenagers as he inveighs against a prevailing atmosphere of religious and racial intolerance. To encourage toleration among young teenagers, the documentary was shown in New York City High Schools. In 1971 Sinatra, who was also nominated for the Best Actor award for his role in *The Man With The Golden Arm* (1955), was honored by the Academy Awards with the Jean Hersholt Humanitarian Award for his many charitable works.

Another little-known Italian American Oscar winner was American cartoonist, animator, producer, and director Walter Benjamin Lantz, the son of immigrants Francesco Paolo Lantz (originally Lanza), from southern Italy, and Mary Jarvis (Maria Gervasi), from northern Italy. He was born in New Rochelle, New York in 1899. It was said that the family name, Lanza, was changed to Lantz by an immigration official. Although Walter grew up in a musical household, his preference was for art—he loved to draw and studied art in school until he was needed to help the family and quit formal schooling at age twelve. However, he took a correspondence course in art and continued to draw and teach animation. He attended the New York's Art Students League and worked with fellow Italian American Gregory La Cava, then the Hearst Studio's leading cartoonist and a future famed director. In the late 1920s, Walter moved to Hollywood, where he began making cartoons that appeared in a number of films for various directors, before becoming chief of the animation department at Universal Studios.[6] Enjoying great success as a cartoonist in the movie capital, he founded his own company, Walter Lantz Productions, which operated for many years and was respected because, "His relaxed working environment was a peaceful oasis attracting many excellent artists from other productions companies." This attribute was important in a field where crews working against a deadline for a feature film could include dozens, if not hundreds, of artists working ten to twelve hours a day. It was the Lantz studio that created a number of unforgettable cartoon characters, the most famous of which was Woody Woodpecker.[7] In 1979, he received an Honorary Academy Award for "bringing joy and laughter to every part of the world through his unique animated motion pictures." Walt Disney was the only animator given an Academy Award prior to this.

The Best Actor nominations of two Italian Americans—Robert De Niro (*Taxi Driver*), and Sylvester Stallone (*Rocky*)—as well as that of Italian Giancarlo Giannini (*Seven Beauties*), rendered 1977 a year of special significance because they were three of the five nominees in that category. Even though none of them won that year, their nominations speak volumes regarding their ascendancy in the realm of film and the esteem in which they were held. Furthermore, *Taxi Driver* was nominated for Best Picture but lost to *Rocky,* while *Seven Beauties* was nominated for Best Director, Best Foreign Film, and Best Writing.

In addition to Italian Americans Martin Scorsese, Francis Ford Coppola, and Frank Capra, who directed or produced movies that have resulted in the awarding of multiple Oscars for acting or directing, there are other Italian Americans who received numerous Academy Award nominations in non-acting or -directing roles. Although not nearly as well known as famous Hollywood actors or directors, these behind-the-scenes personnel provide features indispensable to the production of successful and significant movies. As already discussed, musical background suitable to film's story line has been part of moviemaking from its onset—from pianists whose playing supplied the backdrop to silent screen melodramas to modern soundtracks and the crucial part they play in the talking picture era. A case in point is Harry Warren (Salvatore Guaragna) who received Oscar nominations for Best Music eleven times and won three times, for "Lullaby of Broadway" in *Gold Diggers* (1935), "You'll Never Know" in *Hello, Frisco, Hello* (1943), and "On The Atchison, Topeka and the Santa Fe" in *The Harvey Girls* (1949).

Production designers constitute another behind-the-scenes group deserving credit for their important roles in crafting a convincing visual landscape appropriate to the theme of a movie. The best art and set designers have a remarkable eye for detail that is incorporated in a movie production that effectively enables viewers to imagine another time or place. A review of Italian American art and or set designers finds an increase in their appearances as award-winners and especially as nominees. Over a fifty-year career, during which he worked on seventy-six films, Edward C. Carfagno became a highly respected craftsman in the motion-picture industry who built a well-deserved reputation for creating visual concepts and sets for films that retained historical accuracy. He received Oscar nominations for Best Art Direction/Set Design thirteen times and won these awards three times, for *The Bad and the Beautiful* (1952), *Julius Caesar* (1953), and *Ben-Hur* (1959). He died at age eighty-nine, in 1997. Dante Ferretti received six Oscar nominations for Best Art Direction/Set Design—five of them together with Francesca LoSchiavo —while Albert S. D'Agostino was the recipient of five such nominations.

ENDNOTES

1. Tom O'Neil, *Movie Awards* (Berkley: New York, 2001), 5.
2. Pellegrino D'Acierno, *The Italian American Heritage : a Companion to Literature and Arts* (New York: Garland, 1999), 593. See also Mirella Jona Affron, "The Italian American in American Films, 1918–1971," *Italian Americana* 3, no. 2 (Spring/Summer 1977): 233–255.
3. Mark Winokur, *American Laughter: Immigrants, Ethnicity and 1930s Hollywood Film Comedy* (New York: St. Martin's Press, 1996), 83. See Lenburg, *The Encylopedia of Animated Cartoons*, 18, 28, 32 for more info regarding his cartoon career in Hollywood.
4. For further elucidation of the dominance of Italian themes in filmmaking from the 1980s on, see John Paul Russo, "Italian American Filmmakers, No Deal on Madonna Street," *Italian Americana* 13, no. 1 (Winter 1995): 5–8.
5. *New York Times*, March 30, 1993.
6. Otto Bruno, "Cartooning Icon," *Fra Noi*, September 2011, 35–39. See also Joe Adamson, *The Walter Lantz Story : With Woody Woodpecker and Friends* (New York: Putnam Adult, 1985).
7. For information on studio working conditions see, Giannalberto Bendazzi, *Cartoons: One Hundred Years of Animation* (Bloomington: Indiana University Press, 1999), 136. For more on Lantz's career, see Lenburg, *The Encylopedia of Animated Cartoons*, 39–40, 91–92, 103, 138.

CONCLUSION

This book set out to explore the scope, intensity and penetration of Italian Americans into the core of the Hollywood filmmaking enterprise. It examined participation on all levels by Americans of Italian heritage and Italian nationals, from the inception of the movie industry, commencing in the late nineteenth century, into the first decade of the twenty-first century. Accordingly, we have traversed the embryonic era of cinematic endeavor, which witnessed a very small but motivating group of individuals who were active as thespians, directors, and other behind-the-scenes participants, some born in Italy and others American born. In a sense, Hollywood's Italian Americans represented a cross section of American society. Thus, some entered the filmmaking industry quite by accident, while others brought with them a theatrical background formed by Italian family acting traditions or professional stage and opera experience. Some received minimal formal education, while others possessed impressive backgrounds in other professions. Some were encouraged to enter theater by parents and other family members, while others set out on their own to break new ground. While a few came from well-to-do families, most came from more meager economic circumstances. Some derived their livelihoods working as directors, producers, screenwriters, designers, and songwriters, while others became notable character actors and actresses and a remarkable number became leading stars in the fullest sense of filmdom. Although many actors played stereotypical Italian, gangster roles, more than a few, such as Don Ameche, Anne Bancroft, and Philip Bosco, were also cast in nonethnic parts befitting their acting ability. Thus, this work is about more that mafia, mob, and meatballs; it is about scripts, directors, music, costumes, film editing, and the like. In a word, it is about Hollywood and Italian Americans whose portrayals go far beyond the world of violent criminal behavior.

The term Italian Americans is inclusive of Hollywood movie industry people whose ethnic background may have been wholly or partially of Italian ancestry—a phenomenon increasingly apparent in the second half of the twentieth century. Collectively this cohort accounts for approximately five to six percent of the nation's total population, a figure that is significant, although hardly overwhelming. Nevertheless, their participation in the moviemaking industry, while initially very limited, has become so prevalent that it suggests a representation far larger than their percentage of the population. They have moved from the margins of Hollywood's most famous activity to the mainstream—from the periphery to the *prominenti*.

A summary of Oscars presented to Italian Americans and Italians in various categories provides tangible evidence of their extraordinary impact. From the inception of the Academy Awards in 1927 through 2011, there have been eighty-three award ceremonies in which eighty-three Best Picture Awards have been given—fourteen (16.8 percent) of them to movies directed, produced or written by Americans of Italian descent. Nine (10.8 percent) of the eighty-three awards for Best Actor have gone to the Italian ethnic group while five (six percent) Best Actress Awards have been tendered to women in the group. Eleven (13.2 percent) Italian Americans and Italians have won Best Director Awards while the Oscar for Best Foreign Language Film has been awarded to a truly impressive thirteen (15.2 percent) products from Italy. Nine (10.8 percent) Best Music Awards have been awarded to members of the ethnic group as well as five (6 percent) For Original Score, six (7.2 percent) for Best Cinematography, eleven (13.2 percent) for Best Art Direction, eleven (13.2 percent) for Best Costume, six (7.2 percent) for Best Film Editing, seven (8.4 percent) for Best Short Subjects, eight (9.6 percent) for Special Effects, and six (7.2 percent) for Best Sound. In addition, Italians and Italian Americans have received a staggering number of Oscar nominations for different categories. By any measure, these numbers illustrate an influence far beyond their percentage in the total population; in sum, it merits attention as a remarkable coming of age story.

Academy Award Winners

BEST PICTURE

1929 *Seventh Heaven* (Frank Borzage, director)

1931 *Bad Girl* (Frank Borzage, director)

1934 *It Happened One Night* (Frank Capra, director)

1936 *Mr. Deeds Goes to Town* (Frank Capra, director)

1938 *You Can't Take it With You* (Frank Capra, director)

1958 *Gigi* (Vincente Minnelli, director)

1972 *The Godfather* (Francis Ford Coppola, director)

1974 *The Godfather Part II* (Francis Ford Coppola, director)

1976 *Rocky* (Sylvester Stallone, writer)

1995 *Il Postino* (Massimo Troisi, writer)

1996 *The English Patient* (Anthony Minghella, writer, director)

1998 *Life is Beautiful* (Roberto Benigni, writer, director)

2000 *The Gladiator* (David Franzoni, producer, screenplay writer)

2006 *The Departed* (Martin Scorsese, director)

BEST ACTOR

1955 Ernest Borgnine (*Marty*)

1980 Robert De Niro (*Raging Bull*)

1981 Henry Fonda (*On Golden Pond*)

1984 F. Murray Abraham (*Amadeus*)

1992 Al Pacino (*Scent of a Woman*)

1995 Nicholas Cage (*Leaving Las Vegas*)

1998 Roberto Benigni (*Life is Beautiful*)

2003 Sean Penn (*Mystic River*)

2008 Sean Penn (*Milk*)

BEST ACTRESS

1955 Anna Magnani (*The Rose Tattoo*)

1961 Sophia Loren (*Two Women*)

1962 Anne Bancroft (*The Miracle Worker*)

1972 Liza Minnelli (*Cabaret*)

1995 Susan Sarandon (*Dead Man Walking*)

BEST SUPPORTING ACTOR

1953 Frank Sinatra (*From Here to Eternity*)

1974 Robert DeNiro (*The Godfather Part II*)

1990 Joe Pesci (*Goodfellas*)

BEST SUPPORTING ACTRESS

1992 Marisa Tomei (*My Cousin Vinny*)

1995 Mira Sorvino (*Mighty Aphrodite*)

2010 Melissa Leo(*The Fighter*)

BEST DIRECTOR

1929 Frank Borzage (*Seventh Heaven*)

1931 Frank Borzage (*Bad Girl*)

1934 Frank Capra (*It Happened One Night*)

1936 Frank Capra (*Mr. Deeds Goes to Town*)

1938 Frank Capra (*You Can't Take it With You*)

1958 Vincente Minnelli (*Gigi*)

1974 Francis Ford Coppola (*The Godfather Part II*)

1978 Michael Cimino, (*The Deer Hunter*)

1987 Bernardo Bertolucci (*The Last Emperor)*

1996 Anthony Minghella (*The English Patient*)

2006 Martin Scorsese (*The Departed*)

BEST FOREIGN LANGUAGE FILM

1948 *Shoe-shine (Sciuscia,* Vittoio De Sica director, Cesare Zavattini, script). Since the Motion Picture Association did not then have a Best Foreign Language Film category this movie received an Honorary Award.

1949 *Bicycle Thief* (Vittorio De Sica, director)

1950 *The Walls of Malapaga* (Rene Clement, coproduced with France)

1956 *La Strada* (Federico Fellini, director. Dino

De Laurentis, coproducer)

1957 *The Nights of Cabiria* (Federici Fellini,

director, Dino De Laurentis, producer)

1963 *81/2* (Federico Fellini, director)

1964 *Yesterday, Today and Tomorrow* (Vittorio De Sica, director)

1970 *Investigation of a Citizen Above Suspicion* (Elio Petri, director)

1971 *The Garden of the Finzi Continis* (Vittorio De Sica, director)

1973 *Amarcord* (Federico Fellini, director)

1988 *Cinema Paradiso* (Giuseppe Tornatore, director)

1991 *Mediterraneo* (Gabrielle Salvatores, director)

1997 *Life is Beautiful* (Roberto Benigno, director)

N.B. In addition to the winners, 15 additional Italian-produced movies were nominated for Best Foreign Language Film Oscars.

BEST ORIGINAL SCREENPLAY

1970 Francis Ford Coppola and cowriter Edmund H. North (*Patton*)

1994 Quentin Tarantino (*Pulp Fiction*)

2003 Sofia Coppola (*Lost in Translation*)

BEST SCREENPLAY ADAPTATION

1972 Mario Puzo and Francis Ford Coppola, (*The

Godfather)*

Best Dramatic Screenplay 1997 *Life is Beautiful* (Roberto Benigno)

MUSIC

Best Song
1935 "Lullaby of Broadway" (*Gold Diggers of 1935*) Harry Warren and Al Dubin.

1943 "You'll Never Know" (*Hello, Frisco, Hello*) Harry Warren and Mack Gordon.

1946 "On the Atchison, Topeka and the Santa Fe" (*The Harvey Girls*) Harry Warren and Johnny Mercer.

1961 "Moon River" (*Breakfast at Tiffany's*) Henry Mancini

with Johnny Mercer

1962 "Days of Wine and Roses" (*Days of Wine and Roses*) Henry Mancini

1983 "Flashdance…What a Feeling" (*Flashdance*) Giorgio Moroder.

1986 "Take My Breath Away" (*Top Gun*) Giorgio Moroder.

1987 "(I've Had) The Time of My Life" (*Dirty Dancing*) Franke Previte, John DeNicola and Donald Markowitz

1993 "Streets of Philadelphia" (*Philadelphia*) Bruce Springsteen

BEST ORIGINAL SONG/SCORE
1978 Giorgio Moroder (*Midnight Express*)

1983 Henry Mancini (*Victoria, Victoria*)

1974 Nino Rota and Carmine Coppola (*The Godfather Part II*)

2007 Dario Marianelli (*Atonement*)

2010 Michael Giacchino (*UP*)

BEST ADAPTATION SCORE
1983 *Victoria, Victoria* (Henry Mancini)

BEST DRAMATIC SCORE
1997 *Life is Beautiful* (Nicola Piovani)

PRODUCERS OF ACADEMY AWARD—WINNING FILMS

1938 Frank Capra (You Can't Take it With You)

1971 Philip D'Antoni (The French Connection)

1965 Carlo Ponti (Doctor Zhivago)

1974 Francis Ford Coppola (The Godfather Part II)

2000 David Franzoni, coproducer (The Gladiator)

HONORARY AWARDS

1946 Frank Sinatra (*The House I Live In*)

1971 Frank Sinatra (Jean Hersholt Humanitarian Award)

1950 Vittorio De Sica, director, Ceasre Zavattini, script (*Bicycle Thief*, Special Honorary Award)

1978 Walter Lantz (Lanza)

1980 Henry Fonda (1905-1982)

1990 Sophia Loren (1934-)

1992 Federico Fellini (1920-1993)

1994 Michelangelo Antonioni (1912-2007)

2006 Ennio Morricone (1928-)

BEST CINEMATOGRAPHY

1936 Gaetano Gaudio (*Anthony Adverse*)

1968 Pasqualino De Santis (*Romeo and Juliet*)

1979 Vittorio Storaro (*Apocalypse Now*)

1981 Vittorio Storaro (*Reds*)

1987 Vittorio Storaro (The Last Emperor)

Mauro Fiore (*Avatar*)

BEST ART DIRECTOR

1952 Edward C. Carfagno (*The Bad and the Beautiful*)

1953 Edward C. Carfagno (*Julius Caesar*)

1959 Edward C. Carfagno (*Ben Hur*)

1962 Dario Simoni (*Lawrence of Arabia*)

1965 Dario Simoni (*Doctor Zhivago*)

1986 Gianni Quaranta (*A Room With a View*)

1987 Fernando Scarfiotti, Bruno Cesari, Osvaldo Desideri (*The Last Emperor*)

1992 Luciana Arrighi (*Howards End*)

1995 Eugenio Zanetti (*Restoration)*

2004 Dante Ferretti (*The Aviator)*

2007 Dante Ferretti (*Sweeney Todd)*

BEST COSTUME

1961 Piero Gherardi (*La Dolce Vita*)

1963 Vittorio Nino Novarese (*Cleopatra*)

1964 Piero Gherardi (*8 ½*)

1968 Danilo Donati (*Romeo and Juliet*)

1970 Vittorio Nino Novarese (*Cromwell*)

1975 Milena Canonero (*Barry Lyndon*)

1976 Danilo Donati (*Fellini's Casanova*)

1981 Milena Canonero (*Chariots of Fire*)

1990 Franca Squarciapino (*Cyrano de Bergerac*)

1993, Gabriela Pescucci (*The Age of Innocence*)

2006 Milena Canonero (*Marie Antoinette*)

BEST WRITING

1962 Story and Screenplay Ennio de Concini, Alfredo Giannetti and Pietro Germi (*Divorce Italian Style*)

1963 Pasquale Festa Campanile, Massimo Franciosa, Vasco Pratolini and Nanni Loy, story; Pasquale Festa Campanile, Massimo Franciosa, Nanni Loy and James R. Webb (*How the West Was Won*)

1987 Bernardo Bartolucci (*The Last Emperor*)

ORIGINAL SCREENPLAY

1970 Francis Ford Coppola and cowriter Edmund H. North (*Patton*)

1994 Quentin Tarantino (*Pulp Fiction*)

2003 Sofia Coppola (*Lost in Translation*)

2005 Bobby Moresco (*Crash*)

Screenplay Adaptation 1972 Mario Puzo and Francis Ford Coppola (*The Godfather*)

BEST FILM EDITING

1956 Gene Ruggiero (Around The World in Eighty Days)

1966 Frank Santillo (Grand Prix)

1987 Gabriella Cristiani (The Last Emperor)

1991 Pietro Scalia (JFK)

2000 Stephen Mirrione (Traffic)

2001 Pietro Scalia (Black Hawk Down)

SHORT SUBJECTS

1943 *Yankee Doodle Mouse* (Joseph Barbera and William Hanna, accepted by Frederic Quimby)

1944 *Mouse Trouble* (Joseph Barbera and William Hanna, accepted by Frederic Quimby)

1945 *Quiet Please* (Joseph Barbera and William Hanna, accepted by Frederic Quimby)

1946 *The Cat Concerto* (Joseph Barbera and William Hanna, accepted by Frederic Quimby)

1948 *The Little Orphan* (Joseph Barbera and William Hanna, accepted by Frederic Quimby)

1951 *Two Mouseketeers* (Joseph Barbera and William Hanna, accepted by Frederic Quimby)

1952 *Johann Mouse* (Joseph Barbera and William Hanna, accepted by Frederic Quimby)

SPECIAL EFFECTS

1980 Carlo Rambaldi (*Alien*)

1982 Carlo Rambaldi (*E.T. the Extra Terrestrial*)

1989 John Bruno (*The Abyss*)

1993 Michael Lantieri (*Jurassic Park*)

2003 Joe Letteri (*The Lord of the Rings: The Two Towers*)

2004 Joe Letteri (*The Lord of the Rings: The Return of the King*)

2006 Joe Letteri (*King Kong*)

2010 Joe Letteri (*Avatar*)

BEST SOUND

1976 Arthur Piantadosi (*All the President's Men*)

1982 Gene Cantamessa (*E.T. the Extra-Terrestrial*)

1997 Mark Ulano (Titanic)

2003 Dominic Tavella (*Chicago*)

2004 Steve Cantamessa (Ray)

2010 Gary A. Rizzo (Inception)

BEST VISUAL EFFECTS

1957 Walter Rossi (*The Enemy Below*)

Robert Legato (*Titanic*)

IRVING G. THALBERG MEMORIAL AWARD

1982: Albert R. Broccoli

2001: Dino De Laurentiis

2010: Francis Ford Coppola

NOTABLE ACADEMY AWARD NOMINATIONS
(FOR NINE CATEGORIES)

BEST PICTURE
1931 Bad Girl (Frank Borzage)

1933 *Lady for a Day* (Frank Capra)

1936 *Mr. Deeds Goes to Town* (Frank Capra)

1937 *Lost Horizon* (Frank Capra)

1937 *Stage Door* (Gregory LaCava)

1939 *Mr. Smith Goes to Washington* (Frank Capra)

1946 *It's a Wonderful Life* (Frank Capra)

1950 *Father of the Bride* (Vincente Minnelli)

1961 *Pocketful of Miracles* (Frank Capra) also garnered Academy Award nominations for Best Costume Design, Best Song, and Best Supporting Actor

1974 *The Conversation* (Francis Ford Coppola)

1975 *Taxi Driver* (Martin Scorsese)

1986 *The Mission* (Fernando Ghia, producer)

1990 *Awakenings* (directed and coproduced by Penny Marshall)

1990 *Goodfellas* (Martin Scorsese, director)

1990 *Pretty Woman* (Garry Marshall, producer)

1990 *The Godfather, Part III* (Francis Ford Coppola, director)

1995 *Pulp Fiction* (Quentin Tarantino)

1995 *Il Postino* (Mario Cecchi Gori, Vittorio Cecchi Gori, Gaetano Daniele, producers)

1997 *The Full Monty* (Peter Cattaneo, director)

1998 *Life is Beautiful* (Roberto Benigni, writer, director)

2002 *Gangs of New York* (Martin Scorsese)

2003 *Lost In Translation* (Sofia Coppola)

2009 *Inglorious Basterds* (Quentin Tarentino, director)

2011 *The Social Network* (Dana Brunetti, Michael De Luca, coproducers)

BEST ACTOR

1940 Henry Fonda (*The Grapes of Wrath*)

1955 Frank Sinatra (*The Man With The Golden Arm*)

1957 Anthony Franciosa (*A Hatful of Rain*)

1962 Marcello Mastroianni (*Divorce Italian Style*)

1973 Al Pacino (*Serpico*)

1974 Al Pacino (*The Godfather, Part II*)

1975 Al Pacino (*Dog Day Afternoon*)

1976 Robert De Niro (*Taxi Driver*)

1976 Giancarlo Giannini (*Seven Beauties*)

1976 Sylvester Stallone (*Rocky*)

1977 John Travolta (*Saturday Night Fever*)

1977 Marcello Mastroianni (*A Special Day*)

1978 Robet DeNiro (*The Deer Hunter*)

1979 Al Pacino (*And Justice For All*)

1987 Marcello Mastroianni (*Dark Eyes*)

1983 Tom Conti (*Reuben, Reuben*)

1990 Robert DeNiro (*Awakenings*)

1991 Robert De Niro (*Cape Fear*)

1994 John Travolta (*Pulp Fiction)*

1994 Massimo Troisi (*Il Postino*) a posthumous nomination

1995 Sean Penn *(Dead Man Walking*)

1999 Sean Penn (*Sweet and Lowdown*)

2001 Sean Penn (*I Am Sam Maverick*)

2002 Nicolas Cage (*Adaptation*)

2004 Leonardo DiCaprio (*The Aviator*)

2006 Leonardo DiCaprio (*Blood Diamond*)

2008 Frank Langella (*Frost/Nixon*)

BEST ACTRESS

1957 Anna Magnani (*Wild is the Wind*)

1964 Sophia Loren in (*Marriage Italian Style*)

1964 Anne Bancroft (*The Pumpkin Eater*)

1967 Anne Bancroft (*The Graduate*)

1969 Liza Minnelli (*The Sterile Cuckoo*)

1976 Talia Shire (*Rocky*)

1977 Anne Bancroft (*The Miracle Worker*)

1981 Susan Sarandon (*Atlantic City*)

1985 Anne Bancroft (*Agnes of God*)

1989 Angelica Huston (*Enemies, a Love Story*)

1990 Angelica Huston (*The Grifters*)

1991 Susan Sarandon in (*Thelma & Louise*)

1992 Susan Sarandon (*Lorenzo's Oil*)

1994 Susan Sarandon (*The Client*)

2008 Melissa Leo (*Frozen River*)

BEST SUPPORTING ACTOR

1955 Sal Mineo (*Rebel Without a Cause*)

1957 Vittorio De Sica (*A Farewell to Arms*)

1960 Sal Mineo (*Exodus*)

1962 Victor Buono (*Whatever Happened to Baby Jane?*)

1963 Bobby Darin (*Captain Newman, M.D.*)

1970 Richard Castellano (*Lovers and Other Strangers*)

1972 Al Pacino (*The Godfather*)

1973 Vincent Gardenia (*Bang the Drum Slowly*)

1974 Michael V. Gazzo (*The Godfather, Part II*)

1976 Burt Young (*Rocky*)

1980 Joe Pesci (*Raging Bull*)

1981 James Coco (*Only When I Laugh*)

1985 Robert Loggia (*Jagged Edge*)

1987 Vincent Gardenia (*Moonstruck*)

1989 Danny Aiello (*Do the Right Thing*)

1990 Joe Pesci (*Goodfellas*)

1990 Al Pacino (*Dick Tracy*)

1992 Al Pacino (*Glengarry Glen Ross*)

1994 Leonardo DiCaprio (*What's Eating Gilbert Grape?*)

1994 Gary Sinise (*Forrest Gump*)

1994 Chazz Palminteri (*Bullets Over Broadway*)

2004 Alan Alda (*The Aviator*)

2005 Paul Giamatti (*Cinderella Man*)

2009 Stanley Tucci (*The Lovely Bones*)

2010 Mark Ruffalo (*The Kids Are All Right*)

BEST SUPPORTING ACTRESS

1955 Marisa Pavan (*The Rose Tattoo*)

1956 Patty McCormack, child star (*The Bad Seed*)

1963 Diane Cilento (*Tom Jones*)

1974 Talia Shire (*The Godfather Part II*)

1974 Valentina Cortese (*Day for Night*)

1975 Brenda Vaccaro (*Once is Not Enough*)

1985 Angelica Huston (*Prizzi's Honor*)

1986 Mary Elizabeth Mastrantonio (*The Color of Money*)

1990 Lorraine Bracco (*Goodfellas*)

2001 Marisa Tomei (*In the Bedroom*)

2009 Marisa Tomei (*The Wrestler*)

BEST DIRECTOR

1932-3 Frank Capra (*Lady For a Day*)

1936 Gregory La Cava (*My Man Godfrey*)

1937 Gregory La Cava (*Stage Door*)

1939 Frank Capra (*Mr. Smith Goes to Washington*)

1946 Frank Capra (*It's a Wonderful Life*)

1951 Vincente Minnelli (*An American in Paris*)

1951 Vincente Minnelli (*Gigi*)

1960 Federico Fellini (*La Dolce Vita*)

1962 Pietro Germi (*Divorce Italian Style*)

1963 Federico Fellini (*8 ½*)

1966 Michelangelo Antonioni (*Blow-up*)

1967 Federico Fellini (*Fellini Satyricon*)

1968 Franco Zeffirelli (*Romeo and Juliet*)

1968 Gillo Pontecorvo (*The Battle of Algiers*)

1972 Francis Ford Coppola (*The Godfather*)

1973 Bernardo Bertolucci (*Last Tango in Paris*)

1975 Federico Fellini (*Amarcord*)

1975 Lina Wertmuller (*Seven Beauties*)

1979 Francis Ford Coppola (*Apocalypse Now*)

1980 Martin Scorsese (*Raging Bull*)

1987 Bernardo Bertolucci (*The Last Emperor*)

1988 Martin Scorsese (*The Last Temptation of Christ*)

1990 Martin Scorsese (*Goodfellas*)

1990 Francis Ford Coppola (*The Godfather Part III*)

1994 Quentin Tarantino (*Pulp Fiction*)

1997 Peter Cattaneo (*The Full Monty*)

1998 Roberto Benigni (*Life is Beautiful*)

2002 Martin Scorsese (*Gangs of New York*)

2003 Sofia Coppola (*Lost In Translation*)

2004 Martin Scorsese (*The Aviator*)

2009 Quentin Tarantino (*Inglourious Basterds*)

BEST WRITING, STORY OR SCREENPLAY

1939 Frank Capra (*Mr. Smith Goes to Washington*) Best Screenplay

1945 Federico Fellini and Sergio Amidei (*Open City*, Roberto Rossellini, director)

1946 Federico Fellini (*Paisà*, Roberto Rossellini, director)

1953 Federico Fellini (*Il Vitelloni*) Best Writing, Story and Screenplay

1960 Federico Fellini (*La Dolce Vita*) Best Writing, Story and Screenplay - Written Directly for the Screen

1966 Michelangelo Antonioni (*Blow Up*, Carlo Ponti, producer)

1974 Francis Ford Coppola (*The Conversation*) Best Picture, Best Sound, Best Original Screenplay

1976 Federico Fellini and Tonino Guerra (*Amarcord*) Best Original Screenplay

1975 Lina Wertmuller (*Seven Beauties*) Best Actor, Best Director, Best Foreign Language Film, Best Original Screenplay

1997 Roberto Benigni (*Life is Beautiful*) Directing, Film Editing, Best Original Screenplay, Best Picture)

2003 Sofia Coppola (*Lost in Translation*)

> Italy has produced more Best Foreign Language Film Academy Award–winning films than any other country: thirteen, while twenty-seven of its productions have received nomination in this category. Listed below are eighteen Italian-made films that were nominated in the Best Foreign Language Film category. Twenty additional Italian-made films were submitted but did not receive official nominations.

BEST FOREIGN LANGUAGE FILM

1958 *Big Deal on Madonna Street* (Mario Monicelli)

1958 *The Usual Unidentified Thieves* (Mario Monicelli)

1959 *The Great War* (Mario Monicelli)

1960 *Kapo* (Gillo Pontecorvo)

1962 *The Four Days of Naples* (Nanni Loy)

1965 *Marriage Italian Style* (Vittorio De Sica)

1966 *The Battle of Algiers* (Gillo Pontecorvo)

1968 *The Girl With The Pistol* (Mario Monicelli)

1975 *Scent of a Woman* (Dino Risi)

1976 *Seven Beauties* (Lina Wertmuller)

1977 A Special Day (Ettore Scola)

1978 *Viva Italia* (Mario Monicelli, Dino Risi, Ettore Scola)

1979 *To Forget Venice* (Franco Brusati)

1981 *Three Brothers* (Francesco Rosi)

1987 *The Family* (Ettore Scola)

1990 *Open Doors* (Gianni Amelio)

1995 *The Star Maker* (Giuseppe Tornatore)

2005 *Don't Tell* (Cristina Comencini)

BEST ART/SET DESIGN

1936 Alfred S. D'Agostino (*The Magnificent Brute*)

1942 Alfred S. D'Agostino (*The Magnificent Ambersons*)

1943 Alfred S. D'Agostino (*Flight for Freedom*)

1944 Albert S. D'Agostino (*Step Lively*)

1945 Alfred S. D'Agostino (*Experiment Perilous*)

1952 Edward C. Carfagno (*Quo Vadis*)

1954 Edward C. Carfagno (*The Story of Three Loves*)

1955 Edward C. Carfagno (Executive Suite)

1961 Piero Gherardi (*La Dolce Vita*)

1962 Edward C. Carfagno (*Period of Adjustment*)

1963 Edward C. Carfagno (*The Wonderful World of the Brothers Grimm*)

1963 Piero Gherardi (*8 1/2*)

1966 Piero Gherardi (*Juliet of the Spirits*)

1967 Mario Chiari (*Doctor Dolittle*)

1967 Renzo Mongiardino, Dario Simone, Luigi Gervasi (*The Taming of the Shrew*)

1968 Edward Carfagno (*The Shoes of the Fishermen*)

1975 Edward Carfagno (*The Hindenburg*)

1977 Daniel A. Lomino (*Close Encounters of the Third Kind*)

1982 Franco Zeffirelli (*La Traviata*)

1987 Santo Loquasto, George Detitta (*Radio Days*)

1983 Santo Loquasto (*Zelig*)

1989 Dante Ferretti, Francesca LoSchiavo (*The Advewntures of Baron Munchausen*)

1990 Ezio Frigerio (*Cyrano de Bergerac*)

1990 Dante Ferretti, Francesca LoSchiavo (*Hamlet*)

1992 Ferdinando Scarfioti (*Toys*)

1993 Dante Ferretti, Robert Franco (*The Age of Innocence*)

1993 Luciana Arrighi (*The Remains of the Day*)

1994 Santo Loquasto (*Bullets Over Broadway*)

1994 Dante Ferretti, Francesca LoSchiavo (*Interview With a Vampire*)

1997 Dante Ferretti, Francesca LoSchiavo (*Kundun*)

1998 Eugenio Zanetti (*What Dreams May Come*)

1999 Luciana Arrighi (*Anna and the King*)

1999 Bruno Cestari (*The Talented Mr Ripley*)

1999 Beth Rubino (*Cider House Rules*)

2002 Dante Ferretti, Francesca LoSchiavo (*Gangs of New York*)

2005 Jan Pascale (*Good Night, Good Luck*)

2006 Julie Occhipinti (*The Prestige*)

2007 Beth Rubino (*American Gangster*)

2009 Anastasia Masaro (*The Imaginarium of Dr. Parnassus*)

2009 Antonella Cannarozzi (*I Am Love*)

ENDNOTES

1. In addition, Piantadosi was nominated for the Academy Awards Best Sound category for six other movies.

SELECTED BIBLIOGRAPHY

The bibliographic references constitute an eclectic mixture of sources that have been researched and used to write this work. Included are scholarly tomes that meet high standards of scholarship and which are most appropriate in recounting the history of Hollywood's Italians. While others listed may be more casual and in the popular vein, used judiciously they contribute to the unfolding story.

Adamson, Joe. *The Walter Lantz Story : With Woody Woodpecker and Friends*. New York: Putnam Adult, 1985.

Adler, Stella *The Art of Acting*. Edited by Howard Kissel. New York: Applause Books, 2000.

Aleandri, Emelise. *The Italian American Immigrant Theater in New York City*. Charleston, South Carolina, Arcadia, 1999.

Allen, Jane. *Pier Angeli: A Fragile Life*. Jefferson, North Carolina: MacFarland, 2002.

Baker, Aaron. *Contesting Identities, Sports in American Film*. Urbana: University of Illinois Press, 2003.

Bakish, David, *Jimmy Durante: His Show Business Career with an Annotated Bibliography and Discography*. Jefferson, North Carolina: McFarland, 2007.

Ballard, Kaye, and Jim Hessleman. *How I Lost Ten Pounds in 53 Years*. Watson-Guptill: New York, 2006.

Beltran, Mary. *Mixed Race Hollywood*. New York: New York University Press, 2008.

Bendazzi, Giannalberto. *Cartoons: One Hundred Years of Animation*. Bloomington: Indiana University Press, 1999.

Bertellini, Giorgio. *Italy in Early American Cinema*: *Race, Landscape and the Picturesque*. Bloomington: Indiana University Press, 2010.

Bertinelli, Valerie. *Losing it: And Gaining My Life Back One Pound at a Time*. New York: Free Press, 2008.

Bloom, Ken, Michael Feinstein. *The American Songbook: The Singers, Songwriters & The Songs*. New York: Black Dog & Leventhal, 2005.

Bondanella, Peter. *Hollywood Italians*. New York: Continuum, 2004.

Boulard, Gary. *Louis Prima: Music in American Life*. Urbana: University of Illinois Press, 2002.

Bower, Anne, L. *Reel food: Essays on Food and Film*. New York: Routledge, 2004.

Brady, Kathleen, *John Travolta, A Biography.* People Profiles. Bishop Books, 2000.

Broccoli, Albert and Donald Zec. *When The Snow Melts: The Autobiography of Cubby Broccoli*. London: Boxtree Ltd., 1999.

Brunetti, Argentina. *In Sicilian Company*. Albany, Georgia: BearManor Media, 2005.

Capra, Frank. *The Name Above the Title: An Autobiography*. New York: Macmillan, 1971.

Cateura, Linda Brandi. *Growing Up Italian*. New York: William Morrow, 1987.

Catrambo, Gene. *Golden Touch: Frankie Carle*. Roslyn Heights, NY: Libra, 1980.

Celli, Carlo. *National Identities in Global Cinema: How Movies Explain The World*. New York: Palgrave Macmillan. 2011.

Cesari, Armando. *Mario Lanza: An American Tragedy*. Fort Worth, Texas: Baskerville, 2004.

Clavin, Tom. *That Old Black Magic: Louis Prima, Keely Smith, And The Golden Age of Las Vegas.* Chicago: Chicago Review Press, 2010.

Cline, Beverly Fink, *The Lombardo Story*, Don Mills, Ontario: Musson, 1979.

Cook, David A. *A History of Narrative Film.* New York: W.W. Norton, 1990.

Cooke, Mervyn. *A History of Film Music*. New York: Cambridge University Press, 2008.

Costello, Chris, and Raymond Straight. *Lou's on First : a Biography*. New York: St. Martin's Griffin, 1982.

Crown, Lawrence. *Penny Marshall, An UnAuthorized Biography*. Los Angeles: Renaissance Books, 1999.

D'Acierno, Pellegrino. *The Italian American Heritage*: *A Companion to Literature and Arts*. New York: Garland, 1999.

Damone, Vic, and David Chanof. *Singing Was The Easy Part*. New York: St. Martin's Press, 2009.

Deluise, Dom. *Eat This…It'll Make You Feel Better*! New York: Pocket Books, 1990.

Dick, Bernard F.,ed. *Columbia Pictures: Portrait of a Studio*. Lexington, Kentucky: University Press of Kentucky, 1992.

Dougan, Andy. *Untouchable: A Biography of Robert De Niro*. New York, Da Capo Press, 2003.

Dumont, Herve. *Frank Borzage: The Life and Films of a Hollywood Romantic*. Jefferson, North Carolina: McFarland, 2009.

Dyer, Rich. *Nino Rota*: *Film and Feeling*. New York : Palgrave Macmillan on behalf of the British Film Institute, 2010.

Ebert, Roger. *Scorsese by Ebert*. Chicago: University of Chicago Press, 2009.

Faith, William Robert. *Bob Hope: A life in Comedy.* Cambridge, Massachusetts: Da Capo Press, 2003.

Fante, John. *Ask The Dust*. New York: HarperPerennial Modern Classics, 2006.

———. *The John Fante Reader*. Edited by Stephen Cooper. New York: Harper Perennial, 2002.

———. *The Road to Los Angeles*. Santa Rosa: Black Arrow Press, 2000.

Ferry, Jane. *Food in Film: A Culinary Performance of Communication*. New York, Routledge, 2003.

Fonda, Henry, and Howard Teichmann. *Fonda: My Life*. New York: Signet Books, 1982.

Fordin, Hugh. *M-G-M's Greatest Musicals: the Arthur Freed Unit*. New York: Da Capo Press, 1996.

Fowler, Gene. *Schnozzola: The Story of Jimmy Durante*. New York: Viking, 1951.

Francis, Connie. *Who's Sorry Now?*. New York: St. Martin's Press, 1984.

Friedman, Lawrence S. *The Cinema of Martin Scorsese*. New York: Continuum, 1997.

Gardaphe, Fred. *From Wiseguys to Wise Men: The Gangster and Italian American Masculinities*. New York: Routledge, 2006.

Gazzara, Ben. *In The Moment: My Life As An Actor*. New York: Carroll and Graf, 2004.

Girgenti Lane, Antoinette. *Guy Williams: The Man Behind the Mask*. Boalsburg, Pennsylvania: BearManor Media, 2005.

Grobel, Lawrence. *The Unauthorized Biography of Al Pacino*. Leiscester: Charnwood, 2006.

Hamill, Pete. *Why Sinatra Matters*. Boston: Little, Brown, 1999.

Harris, Warren G. *Sophia Loren: A Biography*. New York: Simon & Schuster, 1998.

Herndon, Booton. *The Sweetest Music This Side of Heaven: The Guy Lombardo Story*. New York: McGraw-Hill, 1964.

Holtzman, William. *Seesaw: A Dual Biography of Anne Bancroft and Mel Brooks*. New York: Doubleday, 1979.

Johns, Howard, *Palm Springs Confidential*, Fort Lee, N. J., Barricade Books, 2005.

Kelley, Kitty. *His Way: The Unauthorized Biography of Frank Sinatra*. New York: Bantam, 1987.

Kerr, Walter. *The Silent Clowns*. New York: Da Capo Press, 1990.

Kinn, Gail and Jim Piazza. *The Academy Awards: The Complete Unofficial History*. New York: Black Dog and Leventhal, 2008.

LaGumina, Salvatore J., Frank J. Cavaioli, Salvatore Primeggia, and Joseph A. Varacalli, eds. *The Italian American Experience: An Encyclopedia*. New York: Routledge, 1999.

Landy, Marcia. *Stardom, Italian Style: Screen Performances and Personality in Italian Cinema*. Bloomington: Indiana University Press, 2008.

Lees, Gene. *Did They Mention the Music?* Chicago: Contemporary Books, 1989.

Lenburg, Jeff. *The Encyclopedia of Animated Cartoons*. New York: Facts on File, 1991.

Long, Robert Emmet, and Kate Burton. *Acting: Working in The Theater.* New York: Continuum, 2006.

Lourdeaux, Lee. *Italian and Irish Filmmakers in America: Ford, Capra, Coppola and Scorsese*. Philadelphia: Temple University Press 1993.

Lupone, Patti, and Digby Diehl. *Patti LuPone: A Memoir.* New York: Crown Archetype, 2010.

Mahar, Karen Ward. *Women Filmmakers in Early Hollywood*. Baltimore: Johns Hopkins University Press, 2008.

Marchione, Margherita. *Americans of Italian Heritage*. New York: University Press of America, 1995.

Mariani, John F., and Lidia Bastianich. *How Italian Food Conquered the World*. New York: Palgrave Macmillan, 2011.

Marshall, Garry. *Wake Me When its Funny*: *How to Break into Show Business and Stay There.* New York: Newmarket Press, 1997.

Martin, Deanna. *Memories Are Made of This*: *Through His Daughter's Eyes.* New York: Three Rivers Press, 2004.

McElhaney, Joe. *The Death of Classical Cinema: Lang, Hitchcock, Minnelli*. Albany: SUNY University Press, 2006.

Miller, Randall M., ed. *The Kaleidoscopic Lens: How Hollywood Views Ethnic Groups*. New York: Jerome S. Ozer, 1980.

Monaco, James. *How to Read a Film*. New York: Oxford University Press, 2000.

Ohmart, Ben. *Don Ameche: The Kenosha Comeback Kid*. Albany, Georgia: Bearmanor Media, 2007.

O'Neil, Tom. *Movie Awards*. Berkley: New York, 2001.

Parish, James Roberts. *Hollywood Songsters: Singers Who Act and Actors Who Sing*. New York: Routledge, 2003.

Peary, Gerard. *Quentin Tarantino Interviews*. Jackson: University of Mississippi Press, 1998.

Philips, Gene D. *Godfather*. Lexington, Kentucky: University of Kentucky Press, 2004.

Picerni, Paul, and Tom Weaver. *Steps to Stardom: My Story*. Albany, Georgia, Bear Manor Media, 2007.

Pugliese, Stanislao G. *Frank Sinatra: History, Identity and Italian American Culture*. New York: Palgrave Macmillan, 2004.

Quirk, Lawrence J. *Bob Hope: The Road Well Traveled*. New York: Applause Books, 2000.

Rausch, Andrew J. *The Films of Martin Scorsese and Robert De Niro*. Lanham, Maryland: Scarecrow Press, 2010.

Ricci, Steven. *Cinema and Fascism: Italian Film and Society, 1922-1943*. Berkeley: University of California Press, 2008.

Robson, Eddie. *Coen Brothers*. London: Virgin, 2007.

Rossellini, Isabella. *In The Name of the Father, the Daughters and the Holy Spirits*. London: Haus Publishing, 2006.

Rotella, Mark. *Amore: The Story of the Italian American Song*. New York: Farrar, Straus and Giroux, 2010.

Sanello, Frank. *Stallone: A Rocky Life*. Edinburgh: Mainstream Publishing, 1998.

Schiavelli, Vincent. *Bruculinu, America*. New York: Houghton Miflin, 1998.

Schickel, Richard. *Conversations With Scorsese*. New York: Alfred A. Knopf, 2011.

Server, Lee. *Robert Mitchum*: *Baby, I Don't Care.* New York: St. Martin's Griffin, 2002.

Smith, Emily. *The Sylvester Stallone Handbook: Everything You Need to Know about Sylvester Stallone.* Tebbo, 2011.

Stevens, George, Jr. *Conversations With The Great Movie Makers of Hollywood's Golden Age.* New York: Alfred A. Knopf, 2006.

Thomas, Tony. *Harry Warren and the Hollywood Musical.* Secaucus, New Jersey: Citadel Press, 1975.

Tosches, Nick. *Dino: Living High in the Dirty Business of Dreams.* New York: Delta, 1992.

Welky, David. *The Moguls and the Dictators: Hollywood and the Coming of World War II.*Baltimore: Johns Hopkins University Press, 2008.

Welsh, James M., Gene Phillips, and Rodney F. Hill, *The Francis Ford Coppola Encyclopedia.* Lanham, Maryland: Scarecrow Press, 2010.

Winokur, Mark. *American Laughter: Immigrants, Ethnicity and 1930s Hollywood Film Comedy.* New York: St. Martin's Press, 1996.

INDEX

www.ingramcontent.com/pod-product-compliance
Lightning Source LLC
Chambersburg PA
CBHW031556280326
41928CB00049BA/887